Cobblers to the Council

Anthony Martin

Anthony Martin
E-mail: anthony.martin1@btinternet.com

First Published 2004

ISBN **0-9547415-0-1**
Printed and bound in Great Britain

Contents

Introduction

If Tony Blair was knocked down by a bus today, who would Labour Party members vote for as their next leader? Answer ...the bus driver, probably.

Please note that there are instances of strong language in this book, and I apologise in advance if these cause offence to the reader. Remember that we are documenting a story of local politics conducted at the level of the gutter and in order for it to be an accurate record of what went on, the language used needs to reflect that fact. Accordingly if you are easily offended by strong language then I must caution you against reading this book any further.

This is a book that the Labour Government do not want you to read, and are doing their best to prevent publication. They have a very good reason for this, because inside these pages there are so many things that have been covered up that need to be brought out into the open. Where you start is up to you, but if you just want to laugh at the bizarre sexual antics of some of our Durham City Councillors then go straight to Chapter 1. In Chapter 5 you will find a multi-million pound scandal, bigger than Poulson, bigger than Donnygate, just waiting to be investigated.

The chapter that affected me most personally is Chapter 9, Death on the Tyne, because it tells you about a horrific double murder that could have been avoided and was only allowed to happen because senior people in the Labour Party were more concerned about the party's reputation than the lives of ordinary people. Read "Anatomy of a Stitch-up" before consulting any solicitor or similar professional. Do not read "A Law Unto Themselves" if you want to maintain the comfortable illusion that our legal system is there to punish criminals and protect innocent citizens from injustice.

This is the true story of a remarkable man called Tony Martin (aka The Durham Cobbler,) the man that the local Labour Party came to hate even more than Margaret Thatcher, even though the Cobbler has no interest in politics and has never voted in his life. The conflict started for business reasons when Labour-controlled Durham City Council tried to close his cobbler's shop down. As you will find out if you read the book instead of the council closing his shop down, the Cobbler ended up closing down Labour-controlled Durham City Council. The Prince Bishop's Shopping Centre paid to have double yellow lines in Claypath that caused a dramatic reduction in the Cobbler's trade, and closed every shop in the street apart from his. Even disabled parking was taken away, and the area patrolled aggressively by

Durham Traffic Wardens, creating the infamous "Parking Desert" When Tony the Cobbler finally managed to get a meeting with Legal Department Head Peter Broome and Chief Executive of Durham City Council, Colin Shearsmith, an initially cordial meeting soon degenerated. It was at this time that Shearsmith spoke the words that are likely to haunt him forever. **"What's a back-street cobbler like you going to do to us, then?"** The rest is history.

This is not a book with a happy ending where the good guy beats the bad guys, gets the pretty girl and they both ride off into the sunset. If that is the sort of thing you enjoy then close this book now and look for the section entitled "Mills & Boon." This is a true-life story of a man battling against institutional corruption, where the law and the surrounding organisations are being used to shield criminals and deny justice to ordinary people. As I researched this book I soon grew to realise that the goings-on in Durham City are by no means unique, and the same sort of thing seems to be happening in town halls up and down the country.

What is different about Durham is that not every town has somebody like the Cobbler with the courage to stand up against institutionalised corruption, crime and maladministration, and the ultimate aim of this book is to encourage others to do so. The Town-Hall criminals rely upon the fact that their victims are isolated individuals who are forced to stand alone against their entrenched power. It is my belief that if the electorate knew about the full extent of political corruption in this country there would be a national scandal bigger than anything that has gone before.

Sleaze allegations destroyed the Conservative government, but their corruption was limited to cash-for-questions and a few ministers being caught with their trousers around their ankles at the wrong time. New Labour seems to have turned political corruption into the foundation of their party. To quote Paul Foot in his Private Eye article documenting a PFI tax avoidance scam at the Inland Revenue that had been covered up by Gordon Brown and John Prescott, **"This story, however, is far worse than any sleaze exposed under the Tories"** and goes on **"The frightening probability remains that such things go on all the time, and no one knows about them."**

Most of this book was written in the last half of 2003, which might just turn out to have been a watershed for New Labour. I have tried to write it with national events of this year such as the War in Iraq and its aftermath, the Hutton Inquiry, the Tory leadership challenge and George W. Bush's visit to Sedgefield as a background. It started off with the chapters being in rough chronological order but so much new

4

material became available in the last three months of that year that I was forced to carry out daily rewrites, so I apologise for the fact that the chronology seems to jump about a bit as you read it. The Cobbler's story developed along a lot of different lines as I tried to write it, so it is probably best to treat each chapter as a theme within that story. For instance "A Law Unto Themselves" is the story of Tony's problems with Durham Police, "That's Entertainment" is about his attempt to publicise the scandal of the Gala Theatre, and so on.

Tony the Cobbler asked me to write his story on Thursday May 8th 2003. I remember that day well because it was the day that the Durham Advertiser dropped through my door with the headline "Lib-Dems seize power." It was then that the alarm bells must have started to ring in Labour North, because this was the worst result of a very bad election night for them. If Durham City Council, at the centre of Labour's heartland could be lost to the Liberal Democrats, then anything could happen in the future.

Ex-Durham City Council Leader Maurice Crathorne, infamous for cancelling the City's Meals-on-Wheels scheme to fund a 20% pay rise for City Council Officers, could not understand why it had happened. " I think we did a tremendous job" he is quoted as saying. Not many shared his opinion because he had just delivered the worst electoral result for Labour in Durham City for at least thirty years. The day after the election a City Council employee came into the Cobbler's shop saying that he did not know that Council Officers like animals so much. When asked what he meant, he told how he had seen one of them creeping out of the City Council with three large black plastic bin-bags full of hamster bedding the previous night. As you will find out later, according to one important council ex-employee, a great deal of information relating to the workings of the Council has subsequently disappeared, and one possible explanation is that this vital evidence now sleeps with the hamsters.

It is difficult to estimate how much of the local Labour council's downfall was due to Tony Martin's relentless exposure of local Labour Party corruption in his Cobbler's shop window in Claypath, how much was due to the sporadic efforts of the LibDem activists, and how much was simply disillusionment with New Labour nationally. Most people, including prominent local journalists that I have spoken to, believe that it was an anti-Labour rather than a pro-LibDem phenomenon. The local Labour Party themselves were in no doubt that the disaster was entirely the Cobbler's fault. One disappointed ex-councillor who had just been left with more time to spend with his family even went so far as to complain that the Cobbler had an unfair advantage because the Labour Party did not have a centrally placed shop window to display propaganda in the city centre. Come on guys, that is not quite true. You used to have the Labour Club almost opposite the Cobbler's shop, but your members stopped going in there because of all the hypocrisy that was preached in it so it was forced to close down.

In the aftermath of the bloodbath, Labour North Regional Organiser Mick Hills was called in to carry out an inquest into the electoral disaster of May 1st 2003, and Labour Party activists tell us that he wanted to send some of his people to talk to the Cobbler, but it never happened. It is believed that intervention from the very top of the party prevented this. Mick Hills had come to realise just how dangerous the Cobbler was to Labour's chances of a third term of government because if the knowledge in the Cobbler's head came to the attention of the general public, Labour was in danger of becoming unelectable for a whole generation. Until that time talking to the Cobbler was regarded as a treasonable act for Labour Party members. Sadly for New Labour a lot of disillusioned activists did take that short walk across the street from the Labour Club to the Cobbler's shop to pass on information in spite of all of the threats, and this book is the result.

Tony Martin's story as he told it to me is funny in some parts and sad in others. If by the time you finish reading it you are not convinced that this is the story of a very brave man, then that is the fault of me as a writer rather than Tony as a man. People with the courage to speak out and fight for their beliefs against all the odds are few and far between. They either end up as heroes like Nelson Mandela or they die mysterious premature deaths, and only time will tell which way our story will ultimately end.

There are incidents in this story that are so bizarre the reader might be tempted to believe that it is a work of fiction. Everything in this book is true, except that some of the names have been changed to protect the guilty. As long as Britain has the most draconian libel laws in Europe and a legal system that is geared up to ensure that a rich person will always beat a poor person no matter who is right and who is wrong, sadly this must remain. If a real name is used that means that permission has been given by that person or that name has appeared in a press or TV item.

There are times when I have chosen to highlight the narrative with pieces drawn from my own imagination and I trust that a reasonably intelligent reader can differentiate these "products of a sick mind" (as they have been described) from straightforward story-telling. Believe me, these imaginings are based upon solid research of the subjects in question, and are probably closer to the truth than you might imagine. In fact I might also be prepared to argue that my mind could have become sick because of long-term Labour Party membership and council employment, so be warned lawyers!

The sad thing about this is that the Cobbler is a hard working honest man, who is prepared to stand up for his principles. He is the sort of man that the Labour Party used to have at its foundation. Personally, I believe that if the local Labour Party had removed the double yellow lines that caused the dispute from the outside of Tony's shop they would still be in power in Durham City. Decide for yourself. Read the book.

Finally, there may be bits in this book that might tempt you to laugh at the corruption and incompetence of our Durham City Councillors. As you do so, remember that this is the way that Tony Blair and George W. Bush want to run the whole world. Prior to publication this manuscript was seen by a man whom I believe to be an honest solicitor, who was obviously hurt at my numerous references to those within his profession who are not quite as scrupulous as he is. I thank him for the work he has done in enabling this book to be published, and because of this I hope that in future I may be able to take a more measured view of the work of the legal profession of this country.

However my considered opinion, arrived at over a four-year period of looking at the work of lawyers, police, politicians and trade unionists in and around Durham is that you must treat these people with caution. In particular it is very unwise (IMHO) to give any of these people important original documents without copying them first, and I have numerous examples of people who say that meetings have taken place with these professionals who subsequently deny important promises they have made.

At around £100 a minidisk recorder and microphone is a good investment under these circumstances, as is a few minutes reading "Anatomy of a Stitch-Up" at the end of this book. If you are in a dispute of this sort then good luck to you and keep on fighting, because the one thing that these people want you to believe is that it is hopeless to struggle against their overwhelming odds. Tony Martin, the Durham Cobbler has inspired me to keep on fighting, and has given me back some of my self respect by allowing me to tell his story to you. I thank him for this opportunity and hope that his story will be as much of an inspiration to the readers as he has been to me.

Chapter 1
Sex ....

Cobbling is like sex, the longer you do it the better you become at it. So who would want to go to a shop called "Mister Minute?"

Tony Martin.

Well, that's got your attention, hasn't it? Don't just stand in the bookshop and try to pick out all the best bits. Go on, go over to the till, buy this book and take it home. I promise you that there are some serious bits in the middle about political corruption, but sex sells books like nothing else and the author could really do with some money right now.

In most books the bits with sex in them are spread out so you have to go through it and turn the corners of the pages over so you can come back to them later. For the convenience of our readers we have put all the juicy bits about perverts and paedophiles right at the front. Now all you have to do is skip the first page or so because that is just a bit of padding about the history of the Cobbler's shop and Tony Blair growing up in Durham. If full-blooded bonking-like-rabbits heterosexual sex is what turns you on then you might want to go straight ahead to the bit that starts with the strikingly well-endowed ex-Commonwealth Games athlete in leopardskin briefs screwing his office staff and filming it for his own personal (you know what I mean, wink wink) enjoyment later. There's also a bit about two senior members of Durham City Council caught on film bonking like rabbits on Council premises. Take two pages forward and prepare to be amused.

Serious News of The World readers might want to skip four or five pages to where there is a bit about a paedophile head teacher (a "chicken-rustler" as the gay community call them) whose activities were covered up by a senior Durham Labour politician. Then there's a little bit about a Durham County Councillor who kept getting caught doing silly things in the gents toilets, but we can't really say much about that because it all got covered up and he was let off with a caution

To be honest the rest of the book will be an anti-climax for you (yes, the pun was intended) because it's all about corrupt politicians screwing you out of millions of pounds of tax-money and corrupt policemen covering it all up. There's a semi-serious bit at the back about politicians plotting to take over the world, overthrowing democratic government and killing off most of the poor people, but that is really only intended for people who have some sort of ongoing interest in the future of mankind. If you are tree-hugging Friends of the Earth conspiracy theorist hippie you might want to read some of that stuff. By now I hope you realise that what you are reading is a light-hearted expose of local political corruption. Therefore at this point you have three choices:

1. Put the book down and go to the shelves in the bookshop marked "Kafka" or "Marx" or even "Mills & Boon" because this book is somewhere between these three extremes, and therefore not for you. You cannot please everybody.

2. Skip straight to the dirty bits, as previously described

3. Read a short introduction about Durham City, then go on to the dirty bits

Please make your choice now

Thank you. You have chosen to read the short introduction.

Most of our story takes place in Durham City, which every signpost proudly tells you is the capital of Durham County, Land of the Prince Bishops. Most of the action centres in and around the Cobbler's shop in Claypath, a street more or less at the centre of Durham City, where all compliments, complaints etc regarding this book should be sent. Local historians tell us that there has been a cobbler's shop on this site for hundreds of years, and in days gone by pilgrims who had walked to Durham City to visit the magnificent cathedral would leave their shoes at the shop for repair while they walked the last mile barefoot as a penance. Later they would return for their shoes and pay the cobbler for his services and for hundreds of years people have been grateful for the services of a man who could repair their shoes ravaged by walking on the cobbles of Durham. Eventually of course, like most good things. some politician comes along and messes it all up.

While we are on the subject of politicians messing things up, it is likely that forty years ago you might have seen ten-year old Tony Blair, dressed in his prestigious Durham Chorister School uniform of blazer, grey shorts and purple topped long socks, walking past the Cobbler's shop on his way to school from his home, a whitewashed detached house about 150 yards down the bank close to the present Durham Sixth-Form Centre, near to The Sands. In view of their ex-pupil's subsequent international fame, Chorister School is remarkably non-committal about young Blair. I remember watching a documentary in which his ex-head teacher said something like "He was a splendid boy, the sort that makes up the backbone of any good prep school."

Having met a number of prep-school head teachers in my time I got the distinct impression that this was prep-school head teacher speak for something like "An average sort of boy. I think, nobody ever expected him to amount to much though. In fact, I can't actually remember who he was. I seem to remember meeting his father once I believe, a Tory alderman, a barrister in chambers in Newcastle, as I remember. I do remember young Rowan Atkinson though; he was at Choristers at about the same time. What a character. Oh yes, we are all very proud of him. I've got all his TV programmes on tape. Really funny. Comes back to hand out prizes at our annual award ceremonies, donations, all sorts of things. Nice man. Not like young whatsisname that we were talking about a minute ago. Never seen him for years. No, I blame his wife."

By all accounts this was quite a happy period in his life, but young Blair was less happy when he moved from Choristers to the very strict Fettes public school in Scotland. He even ran away and tried to stow away on an aircraft to get away from it, according to one biography. Would your parents have had to pay a fixed penalty truancy fine if that had happened in 2003, Tony? At Fettes his preoccupation seems to have been with rock music and he had a strong non-conformist streak. At the age of seventeen his loutish behaviour earned him not a swift march to the nearest cash-point for a fixed penalty fine, but a good old fashioned six of the best from his despairing housemaster. Seventeen is an age when most boys are capable of learning through their ears rather than their backsides and Tony seems never to have forgiven the "lousy" teachers for this final insult upon his dignity and has been taking it out on them ever since, or so many in the teaching profession believe.

Durham City lies a few miles from Sedgefield, now most famous as the constituency of the aforementioned Rt. Hon.Tony Blair. Previously Sedgefield was best known for being the site of the biggest mental hospital in County Durham, Sedgefield Asylum. Sedgefield became so closely associated with mental illness that the two came to mean the same thing. Mothers didn't say to their children "You'll drive me mad." Instead they would say "You'll drive me to Sedgefield !" The people of Sedgefield objected to this and the asylum was officially renamed Winterton Mental Hospital. This grim grey building housed the bulk of the mentally ill inhabitants of County Durham for more than thirty years and closed, with many of its inmates becoming part of the Care In The Community initiative at about the same time that Blair became MP. Many of us have since grown to believe that there was a certain bitter irony in this.

Scandal-and-sleaze-only readers begin here.

Fast forward in time now to the late 1990's. New Labour has just won a landslide national election victory, and spirits are high. All is not well at grass-roots level, however. The scene is the Cobbler's shop in Claypath, Durham. This was a particularly bad day if you were in urgent need of a shoe repair, because you could not get into the Cobbler's shop. It was full of reporters fighting for a story. The reason for this sudden rise to fame was the fact that Tony Martin, the owner of the shop, had started publishing pieces of scandal relating to Durham City Council in his shop window if the local press would not publish it. On this occasion the Cobbler had dug up some absolute gems of scandal relating to the activities of the city's Senior Recreation Officer, Keith Walton. They had turned out to be spectacularly true.

Of all the council hangers-on in this book Keith Walton is undoubtedly the most likeable. This guy had a winning smile and a pleasant manner, and was adored and hero-worshipped by the boys and girls of Durham City Amateur Swimming Club where he worked as Chief Coach because of his Commonwealth Games Bronze swimming medal. Indeed the worst you can say about Keith Walton is that he was a likeable rogue, unlike everybody else in this chapter who are not pheasant pluckers at all.

He is also the person in this book where the gap between what was alleged and what can be proved with a sufficient degree of certainty to be published is at its greatest. When this manuscript came back from the lawyers I was forced to take out about two pages of things that staff, particularly female staff, alleged that he had done but did not have documentation to prove it. As you will see later in a document called the "McWilliams Allegations" it is alleged that he was involved in a brawl with his boss Alan Wilson at the International Cross-Country Championships that he organised, and if that is true it certainly fits the pattern of a man who enjoyed life in a macho sort of way. There may also have been minor irregularities in relation to certain of his business activities, but nothing out of the ordinary by Durham City Council standards. Keith Walton's spectacular fall from grace was simply a result of his enormous carnal appetite.

As well as being an athlete in the swimming pool Keith was, by all accounts, a bit of a star in the bedroom as well. Nothing kinky, just straight consensual adult meat & two veg heterosexual sex, as often as he could get it for as long as he could get it, and it seems he was never short of willing partners. The City Council Cloak of Confidentiality still covers a lot of what occurred and it remains uncertain as to how his activities came to light, but come to light they did and the Cobbler published them in his window. The national press caught on to the story, and eventually the truth came out that Keith Walton, Senior Recreation Officer of Durham City Council, was in the habit of seducing his female staff and videotaping himself having sex with them. His locker was searched, and the videotapes found. The national press read the letters S-E-X and the feeding frenzy started.

At the time the scene inside Tony's shop was incredible. Cameramen and reporters were shoulder to shoulder, fighting for space to fire questions at the Cobbler. I arrived at about 11.30 am, and the overall effect was like some bizarre Monty Python sketch.

"He was taping it - have you got pictures of him?"

"Have you seen them - was he well endowed?"

"He wasn't wearing leopard skin briefs, was he? That would make a great front page!"

This had been going on all morning and at that point the Cobbler's patience appeared to snap.

"Who the f*ck are you?" he shouted, pushing his way through the crowd towards the reporter. "What f*cking newspaper are you from?"

"The Sport" answered the bewildered journalist, moving backwards.

"Well f*ck off out of my shop and ask the c*nt yourself." shouted Tony. "He's selling puncture repair kits in the f*cking bike shop across the road!"

At this point they all streamed out of the shop, headed for Cycleforce across the road where Keith Walton had hoped to spend the rest of his retirement in anonymity. Clearly, this was not to be. The Cobbler almost laughed out loud as they all attempted to squeeze through the narrow door of his shop at the same time, streamed across the road and rushed through the door of the bike shop, only to re-emerge thirty seconds later followed by the bellowing, red-faced Keith Walton.

This may sound like something out of the script of a bad BBC sitcom, but it is not. It is a sample of one of the many incidents that eventually led Private Eye to dub Durham City as "The Rottenest Borough in England." You have not heard the best of this story, however. Here it is.

In spite of an admission of gross misconduct **Keith Walton was not sacked from Durham City Council, he was allowed to retire.** The total amount of his Golden Goodbye remains undisclosed to this day. Why was this, you might ask yourself. Indeed, when you read this book you will come to marvel at why so many people committed so many crimes, and yet nobody got sacked. The answer lies in the complicated web of patronage, nepotism and corruption that was Durham City Council. We all know that the most important thing in life is not what you know, but who you know. With Labour-run Durham City Council the most important thing was what you know about who you know.

It is alleged within the ranks of the local Labour Party that Keith Walton was allowed to retire on full pension because in his locker at Durham City Baths a videotape was found where the leading actor was not Keith himself, but two other important City Council personages. There, immortalised on videotape, humping and moaning in a jacuzzi like horrible old walruses, were two very important senior Labour Party members (who for the time being must remain anonymous) enjoying the hospitality extended to them by their Senior Recreation Officer, blissfully unaware of his recent interest in video photography.

Knowing these two old wrinklies as I do, I find it hard to believe that Keith would want to keep a recording of their activities for his own sexual gratification. These people are not good looking, even with their clothes on. Naked, wet and in the throes of orgasm they must have been a sight more likely to cause you to throw up your lunch than stimulate an erection. Nevertheless possession of evidence like this and threats of its publication would be an embarrassment, even to brass-necked individuals like our unwitting porno-movie stars. Hence Keith Walton's generous pension settlement. Or so the theory goes.

All I can say, Keith, is that if this is true then good luck to you. If you have still got a copy of that tape then let me know and I'll bring a few beers around so we can talk about the good old days because, believe me, that is one home movie that I would most certainly want to see. If you have managed to get one over on these people then you are most certainly my hero!

Name-&-Shame-the-Paedophile readers start here.

Unfortunately other council-related figures enjoyed darker pleasures, and you can be sure that sexual embarrassment followed by cover-up and pensioned retirement was by no means invented for the benefit of Keith Walton. A notable prior example was that of well known ex-head teacher and Labour Party activist ******* ********** Once again, the magic Blanket of Confidentiality covered up the true facts as to what occurred at the infamous camping trip which caused this man to retire from his post as headmaster of ********* School with a nervous breakdown. Nobody ever got to the bottom of it. Getting to the bottom of things was Mr **********'s downfall, according to the parents of the ten-year old boys from the local housing estate who complained after that final camping trip. The Cobbler confronted Keith Mitchell, Director of Education for Durham County Council, demanding to know why this man had slipped through the net when he should really be in prison. When Mitchell found out the infamous ex-head teacher was still teaching children how to use computers he became distinctly uneasy and asked what school he was working in, as he believed this man was still a danger to children. He never got around to doing anything tangible though, and sent the Cobbler a letter full of half-truths and bullshit that he sent on to Brian Thisthlethwaite at Labour North. He promised to do something about it, but never did and disappeared from Labour North shortly afterwards.

All that can be said with any degree of certainty is that *******   ********** was a head teacher who retired from head teaching under a cloud of suspicion. Fortunately for him he had powerful friends so everything was covered up and he was awarded the Golden Goodbye. Soon after that he was to be found teaching fellow Labour Party members how to use computers. In return, ******* ********** carried out a lot of computer-related tasks for the Labour Party. Things really came to a head about the time when local parents kicked up a fuss that our ex-head teacher webmaster was allegedly supplying teenage boys with copious amounts of alcohol when he was supposed to be teaching them how to build internet websites at his home. This incident caused so much concern that a letter went around the neighbourhood warning parents about this man's activities. The local Labour Party countered this by saying that nothing against the man had ever been proved. This man is still a prominent member of Durham City Labour Party

The truth is that none of the allegations against him were ever investigated. The Old Boy's network of corrupt trade union officials and politicians closed ranks to prevent it happening.

Another very senior Durham City politician (whom I would love to name but dare not,) is alleged to have had a chequered past as well, as I soon found out when I started to research this book. This man spent some time teaching in various schools around Durham County. My father-in-law worked as a gardener in one of these schools, and I can still remember his stories about the unusual sexual frankness of the staff towards each other, which they seemed to show no fear of expressing even in the presence of children, and the casual thoughtless brutality of the staff towards the pupils whom they seemed to regard as sub-human. What I was totally unprepared for were the stories of ex-pupils and ex-pupils' parents. Their stories of this teacher's brutality, even judged by the standards of the time, made my skin crawl.

There were stories about boys being wrapped in mattresses to drown the screams while they were kicked until bones were broken, and lies told to parents to cover it all up. These ex-pupils were still afraid of this man and his power even thirty years later, and would only talk with great reluctance after several pints of beer. Even senior councillors who held documentation proving these allegations hesitated to talk, knowing what awaited them if they did. The only person who did was a wonderful old lady called Betty Robinson who came into the Cobbler's shop to tell her story.

Sadly Betty is no longer with us, she passed away in summer 2003 very much mourned by her family and neighbours in Carrville, Durham. If there were more people with the courage of Betty Robinson then corrupt politicians would not get their own way quite so easily and I hope that the publication of her story allows her to rest more peacefully. I am sure she would rest even more peacefully if we named and shamed him but I dare not. Most of the members of City of Durham Constituency Labour Party know all about this, but if the people of Durham City knew this man's name they would be horrified.

That is why I was so very surprised when I received that first anonymous phone call, telling me to mind my own business and stop researching this book or I would be exposed as a child abuser.

Right up until that time I thought that child abusers were shielded from exposure in Durham City, and given well-paid jobs in the Labour Party.

It would be nice to end on a lighter note and tell you the story about the County Councillor who was arrested in a public toilet for "cottaging", soliciting for sex with men in the little cubicles. By all accounts this Councillor was caught standing with his feet in a carrier bag while the other sat on the toilet carrying out an act of oral sex on him, which gave the impression (to casual onlookers) of one man having a crap with his week's shopping at his side. This is all right in poncey places like London but a definite vote-loser in North Road, Durham. The fact is that it was all covered up, he got away with a caution and the whole thing blew over, so we can't mention that one.

And then he got caught again doing the same thing! Whoops a-daisy, we all laughed. Yes, this time he's definitely going to be spending his evenings playing Hunt-The-Soap in the showers of Durham Prison. Then it all got covered up and he got let off with a caution again.

So we can't mention that one.

But we all know who it is, don't we?

This, dear readers, concludes our short study of the bizarre mating habits of the Durham Councillor. If you think it is nothing more than a gratuitous exploitation of something that is really only the concern of the individuals themselves then you are quite right, but if Rupert Murdoch can make millions out of that sort of thing why not a little bit for Tony the Cobbler as well. Personal sexual morality is one thing, but when it gets all tied up with the promotion of patronage, double standards and rank hypocrisy of the sort that has been commonplace over the recent past, it needs to be brought out into the open. That is my excuse and I am sticking to it, so there.

Chapter 2
.... Drugs ....

Chief Constable: Did you know that Tony Martin had the sh*t kicked out of him last night?

Assistant Chief Constable: No......... I didn't even know he had been arrested.

Durham City can be a scary place. The tourists who come to see the picture postcard view of Durham Cathedral from Prebends Bridge might think that ours is a city of timeless tranquillity, but some of us who live here have an entirely different perspective. We know that living here can be like walking on thin ice and if you put a foot wrong, perhaps by saying the wrong things about the wrong people, then you fall through the thin covering of justice and civil liberty into a scary, dangerous world where you are completely alone; a place where you can learn things that ordinary people are better off not knowing. This is what the Cobbler started to learn, as bit-by-bit people started to come into his shop telling him about their experiences in Durham City.

The skyline of Durham City is dominated by a cathedral that is a World Heritage site and one of the most famous picture postcard views in the world, but it has given me a creepy sort of feeling ever since I first saw it as a young child. Like many others I have lived in its shadow for nearly all of my life and we often forget that it has not always been regarded as the jewel in the crown of Durham County. It was built by the Norman invaders soon after the Battle of Hastings, and only after they had destroyed the existing Saxon cathedral that stood on the site, which itself probably replaced a much more ancient place of worship.

The grand building we now cherish was built by forced labour under the command of a conquering army, and its scale always tends to reinforce my belief that one of the main reasons for its construction was to demonstrate the power of these conquerors to the local people. In return for their efforts the Normans carried out the most horrible genocide upon the local population that has ever been seen anywhere in this country and during its first century of existence the foundations of the cathedral were literally soaked in blood as the invaders tried to crush the spirit the local Anglo-Saxons. Interestingly Durham is the only county in England where there are no remaining prehistoric standing-stone circles.

Even to this day a great deal of mystery surrounds Durham Cathedral, not the least of which is to do with the mysterious passages that reach out from the cathedral under the river to various locations within the city and houses around Saddler Street. It is not widely known that some of the houses around that area were previously used as dungeons, and I have been told that during recent repair work at the cathedral a wall was accidentally breached and a previously unknown crypt-like area discovered within the foundations.

Eyewitnesses told of bodies, some of them not nearly as old as you might expect, inside this area. The story goes on to say that members of Durham University Potholing Society heard about this discovery and offered to investigate, but their offer was refused. If there is indeed something mysterious underneath Durham Cathedral then powerful people do not seem want to have it investigated. If anybody can verify any part of this story then the author would be grateful to hear about it.

Those who believe in ghosts talk about mysterious goings-on in Room 21 of Durham Castle, now used for student accommodation, and that students are anxious to get into that room but frequently are very soon anxious to move elsewhere. Once again confirmation or denial would be valuable. The next time you take a rowing boat out from Brown Boathouse you might pause to remember the hundreds of people who used these steps to embark on a much sadder journey towards deportation to the colonies for some minor offence or another, and some say that their spirits linger on here.

Tony Martin, the Durham Cobbler, is a very down-to-earth sort of guy who takes a very sceptical view of ghosts, UFO's and conspiracies. This was the attitude he maintained at first when people came into his shop with stories of crooked police and lawyers in Durham City. At first he took these stories with a pinch of salt, because it is difficult to believe people who talk about a city where the police protect the criminals and harass the law abiding unless you have actually experienced that sort of thing yourself. If you are told that Durham is a city where it is difficult to find an honest solicitor, trades unions have been turned against their members by corrupt politicians and councillors who did not abuse their elected offices were branded as outcasts, you hope that it is not true, because if it is, then your whole belief system is turned on its head. It was only when Tony Martin began to experience these things for himself that he began to realise the immensity of the problems that the people of Durham City faced. As a Labour Party member

I only started to realise the scale of the problem when I witnessed the incident I describe next.

The scene was Durham City Labour Club just across the road from the Cobbler's shop and the time was ten o'clock on one of the last Saturdays of the month in autumn 1998. The delegates of City of Durham Constituency Labour Party were angry. The most recent allegations to appear in the Cobbler's Window, that Ron Morrissey, electoral agent for Gerry Steinberg MP and Chairman of the Education Committee of Durham County Council had been caught with his fingers in the till were clearly outrageous. So outrageous that Ron had not even bothered to turn up to defend himself. Ron only rarely turned up to meetings, and when he did so it was never for longer than ten or fifteen minutes before boredom overtook him and he left. The fact that he never changed his clothing for occasions like this only added to the charisma of the larger than life figure. Gardening clothes, jeans, even on one occasion matching Bermuda shorts and shirt were all part of the studied indifference that he practised. He knew he was at the top of the food chain along with Steinberg and Bowman, and this portly, arrogant Ruskin College educated bully regarded the opinions of lesser beings as unimportant.

After all he had John Bowman, fellow Sherburn Labour Party member and Deputy Leader of Durham City Council to defend him. John stood up and told the assembled delegates that the allegations were all nonsense. He was also on the governing body of Sherburn Hospital, and it was simply not true that money was being siphoned off into excessively generous pension funds for Ron and his wife. He himself had looked into the allegations that large sums of money had been taken from Interchurch, a training agency run by Ron, and reinvested in Interchurch (Spain) which had something to do with timeshare apartments. It was a legitimate investment that had gone wrong. Anybody could make the same mistake. Yes, the combined errors had lost approximately three-quarters of a million pounds of taxpayers' money, but that was a relatively small sum of money compared with the annual budgets of the two organisations concerned.

The delegates were satisfied. John Bowman sat down, allowing himself the luxury of brushing his hand against the platinum-blonde bouffant hairdo of Mildred Brown who always sat beside him. The anger of the delegates now focused on the Cobbler, who was obviously trying to smear the good name of an honest comrade. Next to speak was Harry H, a well trusted ex-policeman. It was all the fault of the Cobbler, he said. The delegates roared in approval. The man was obviously crazy to make allegations against a man like Ron Morrisey. Further roars of approval greeted this self-evident truth. So crazy, in fact, that he must be on drugs! The meeting went wild as this final piece of the jigsaw fell into place. Everything was now crystal clear, except for the drops of foaming saliva coming from Harry's excited mouth, which the surrounding delegates did their best to avoid.

Well then if he is on drugs he must be selling them from his shop! Uproar. The relentless logic of Harry's argument was more than enough to convince the delegates of what they must do. Why should this filthy degenerate masquerading as a cobbler be allowed to corrupt our children under our very noses by peddling his filthy drugs to them? Going over there and hanging the bas**rd there and then was too good for him. It was necessary to make an example of him, for the good of the community as a whole. The bloodlust was up, and the fact that there was not a shred of evidence to support the allegations was unimportant. They hadn't bothered about evidence in the past, so why start now? Get the Drug Squad in there, get him raided and let's have him out of there.

It was some time later that somebody somewhere convinced somebody else of the distinct advantage of having evidence of some form of wrongdoing. Even with their extensive network of corrupt contacts a conviction could not be certain. Getting the Drug Squad to raid the place and plant a few packets of Class A narcotics might be good enough for a house in Sherburn Road Estate, but this was a different matter. Tony Martin was well known to hundreds of his customers and dozens of friends and acquaintances. He liked a good drink at a weekend, but there was not the slightest suggestion that he was at all interested in using illegal drugs, let alone selling them. People knew that, and caution was advised.

Someone within the ranks of Durham Constabulary, clearly of above average intelligence for that organisation, pointed out that the Cobbler's Shop was directly opposite the offices of Gerry Steinberg MP. Why not set up a surveillance operation and hope for the best? All you needed was a known drug user to go in there to have his shoes repaired, and you had all the necessary photographic evidence to guarantee a conviction. This was the start of Tony Martin's first brush with The Long Arm Of The Law.

Before you read then next section, I must make something absolutely plain, **I am not somebody who is anti-police.** From what I can see, 95% of all policemen are hard working, honest guys who keep our society working properly. The problem is that the corrupt 5% seem to rise to the top of every force with a frightening inevitability. The good policemen resent it as much as the victims stitched up by the corrupt policeman, but they are in no better position than anyone else to do anything about it. They resent the corrupt who-you-know-not-what-you-know promotion panels, but it takes an exceptionally brave man to speak out about it when your job and the welfare of your family are at stake.

Just to be absolutely sure, I will say it again. Most police are honest. They are doing the hardest job in the country but to paraphrase a remark made about First World War soldiers **"They are lions led by donkeys"**. Corrupt donkeys at that.

Meanwhile, back to the story. The Monday after the Durham Labour Party meeting, strange things started to happen. As Tony closed down his shop to go for a mid-morning bacon sandwich for himself and his father, he noticed the blinds in the room above Gerry Steinberg's office moving, and the silhouette of two men, one of whom appeared to be filming him. Over and over again, as he lifted his head from his work the blinds across the road moved. Closer to lunchtime a policeman who had been coming into the Cobbler's shop since Tony was a lad entered with a worried look on his face.

"Hiyah" said the Cobbler.

"Can't stay" said the copper. "Just called in to tell you to watch it. The Labour Party is after you."

"Is that who is filming me from across the road?" said Tony.

"Drug Squad" the plain-clothes copper replied

"Drugs Squad!" exclaimed Tony in disbelief.

"Just be careful." the policeman said. "Keep an eye on the shoes that come into your shop and check inside every one". An eye winked, and he turned round and was gone.

The telephone rang. On the other end was a prominent Fleet Street journalist. As he listened, Tony's eyes got wider and wider. There had been a meeting of councillors from all over the region and as usual a lot of free alcohol had been consumed. The talk got louder and louder and people had become careless. A Doncaster Councillor had remarked how the Durham Cobbler " was really sticking it up Durham City Council" Two Durham Councillors replied gleefully that this would soon stop because they had mounted a police surveillance operation on him from Gerry Steinberg's office opposite the Cobbler's Shop, and they would soon be sticking it up him. The Doncaster Councillor reported this to the journalist, and the journalist warned the Cobbler.

The Cobbler could not believe what was being said to him. It seemed that he was the only one in the world who did not know there was a plot against him. Was it the intention of corrupt Labour Councillors to fit him up as a drug dealer? At this point, reason appeared to snap and he dashed out of the shop, down the street, up the narrow steps into the Labour Club and burst through the door.

As Tony described the scene to me I could not help visualising a cowboy movie barroom shootout scene, with him as the hero. The only things missing were the six-guns at his hip and the horses tethered outside of Kwikfit in the street below the club. He burst into the room, silhouetted against the sky outside. There was instant pin-drop silence among the scattered groups in the Labour club.

"Have you lot been setting the coppers to spy on me?"

Everywhere, eyes instantly downcast. A gigantic hairy figure with a thick gold chain around its neck rose slowly to its feet and advanced forward in what it believed to be a menacing way. Knuckles dangling centimetres from the dirty red carpet, this guy was a one-man proof of Darwin's theories of evolution. As he got halfway across the room and realised that his enormous beer-belly and multiple chins wobbling as he walked was doing little to intimidate the angry Cobbler, his body language softened and he turned slightly sideways.

"I'm .. er, sorry you'll have to leave you're not a ………

"Where's ********?"** The room became electrified at the mention of the infamous chicken-rustling ex-headteacher. All eyes were now fixed on the Cobbler

Margaret Davies stood up. "He hasn't stolen anything from you, so leave him alone!"

"Who said anything about stealing things? We both know he's done a lot worse than that to children up at that school. Why aren't you doing anything about him? Why are you setting the coppers to spy on me instead?"

"It's not us, go and ask the police yourself" said Margaret

"I will ! " shouted Tony as he turned and bounded down the stairs, muttering about paedophiles, drug squads and what he would do to them when he got his hands on them

The scene now changes to the local police station a few minutes later. The door flies open.

Enter the Demon King.

"Why the f*ck have you lot been spying on me?"

The question rang out through the almost empty police station. The colour drained from the face of the young constable.
"Er…excuse me, I'll go and get the Desk Sergeant" said the young constable, hurrying out with the air of someone who for once was quite pleased to be in a junior position in the office.

"Yes Mr Martin, what can we do for you today?" enquired the Desk Sergeant as he walked in.

"Why are you lot filming me from Steinberg's office across the road from my shop? What am I supposed to have done?"

"Er, I'm sorry Mr Martin, I really don't know what you are talking about." The Desk Sergeant looked around, perhaps hoping that the earth might open and swallow him up to save him from this very embarrassing situation. "If you leave it with me, I'll get back to you. Have we got your number?" The Cobbler turned in disgust and left.

There are days when reality seems to take a turn for the worse, and this was one of them. Tony just managed to get through the cobbler-shop door when his mobile phone rang. The name on the screen said "Maria," Tony's wife.

"Hiya love, how're doing?" Tony said, trying to calm her down.

"Don't hiya-love me Tony. Those letters that came today - I've seen them. They're disgusting. And that stuff on your website. It's all true isn't it. I've been living with a gay paedophile all these years. I'm leaving you. Goodbye"

"Maria, hang on….." Too late, the phone was dead.

"Dad, we're going to have to shut up shop and go home," said Tony."There's a problem at home."

Fortunately the Tyne Tunnel was fairly clear that day, and the journey home was an all-time record. Tony entered the house to an ominous silence. There, on the fridge supported by two duck fridge magnets were the letters. As he opened the first one a picture of a blonde, Nordic-looking young man fluttered to the floor.

"Hello. My name is Giles, and I love to have my bare bottom spanked with a big wooden paddle...." His voice trailed off into silent disbelief.

Trembling with anger he opened the second letter. This time there was no photograph, but instead a strong smell of expensive aftershave wafted towards his nostrils.

"Hello. My name is John. I'm 21 and I have my own sports-car. I have seen your profile in Janus and I'm just dying to meet you......"

"The bast*rds, I'll kill them!" Tony strode over to the phone and dialled his wife's mother's telephone number.

"Hello, is Maria there?......Never mind about that, just put her on.........Hello , Maria. Look, I've seen the letters.....Are you serious?.......Do you really believe I'm queer?........It's those bast*rds at the Council......Yes, I am asking you to believe that.... It's the truth........What?...Don't be so fond.......Listen, this is ridiculous. I'm coming round now." The phone was slammed down, and he was on his way to his mother-in-law's house.

Tony's relationship with his mother-in-law was much like everybody else's. He knew that his mother in law had told Maria when they first got together. "I don't expect it'll last long, and there'll always be a place for you here, pet." She'll be in her element now, thought the Cobbler as he rang the doorbell. Maria appeared at the door momentarily, disappeared and was replaced by her mother. The light of battle was in her eyes and she was clearly ready to defend her brood to the death.

"What do you want, you PERVERT?" The last word was delivered at full volume and echoed down the street.

"Listen, will you just let me in so that we're not discussing this in the middle of the street with all the neighbours watching?" the Cobbler begged.

"No, I bloody will not let you into my house. And I'll tell you something else. If you go anywhere near those bairns I'll bloody CASTRATE YA!   SO THERE"

Bang - the door rocked on its hinges and he was alone in the street. At either side of the house twitching curtains showed that the local Neighbourhood Watch was in action.

The Cobbler hammered on the door again, and once again his infuriated mother-in-law opened it. "Listen, can I not just come in and talk about it?"

"Let him in mother, we've got to get something sorted out here." Maria's voice behind her had a resigned air to it. Reluctantly the Cobbler's mother moved aside and with all the enthusiasm of a lion-tamer entering the cage of a pain-crazed lion, he stepped through the door. Almost before the door was closed the tirade of abuse resumed.

"YOU DIRTY BUGGER! YOU FILTHY PERVERT! She's been telling me all about it! Those things.......disgusting, that's what I say........and those poor bairns.... I knew it.... I knew it all along....I told her...didn't I tell ya...Filthy...filthy...disgusting..." By now her mother's anger had faded to a dull roar, and Maria's voice somehow managed to get through to her

"Mother, look, Tony and I need to talk. Please go and make us a cup of tea." Her mother paused for a moment and eyed the Cobbler. Running her eyes up and down him she seemed somehow to reassure herself that the moment she stepped into the kitchen the Cobbler was unlikely to whisk out a full set of black-leather bondage gear and begin abusing her daughter there and then, and she reluctantly stepped towards the kitchen door, never taking her eyes off the Cobbler, never turning her back to him.

"She's a bit upset," Maria warned. A dozen smart-alec answers immediately crossed the Cobbler's mind, any one of which would have almost certainly caused a catastrophic return of his mother-in -law and an equally certain personal mutilation, because he knew that the kitchen was full of big sharp knives. For once in his life common sense got the better of him and he adopted a low-profile reply

"Listen Maria, I'm so sorry that you've been dragged into this. It's the last thing I wanted, really. Honestly, it's that lot at the Labour Party in Durham they're doing the dirty tricks bit. You know that you're the most important thing in the world to me. You know that I'm not gay. You know I'm not a pervert. I love you. I've always loved you and I'll always love you."

By now Maria's eyes were shining and a small tear was beginning to trickle down the side of her face. Her relationship with the Cobbler had been difficult for a while because things were not going well at the shop in Durham and Tony tended to bring his problems home with him. All was forgiven now though, and these were the words she had wanted to hear for so long. Tearfully she dissolved into his arms and they embraced passionately. Unfortunately her mother chose just this moment to re-enter the room, tea and biscuits on a tray in her hands.

The tray clashed onto the table, spilling tea everywhere. "Get your dirty hands off my daughter, you disgusting filthy PERVERT ! " she screamed, beating her clenched fists on the Cobbler's shoulders. By now the Cobbler's two young sons had managed to venture out of their room and were half way down the stairs, wide eyed and wondering, amazed at the sort of things grown-ups can get up to when there is nobody to tell them what to do.

"Mother, Mother stop it......Tony's explained everything....It's a trick, it's a joke.....Mother, stop it!" Maria's voice cut through her mother's anger and the flailing stopped. She sat down beside the spilt tea tray, wailing in uncertainty and distress. "Mother, it's alright, honestly it's alright, really" Maria reassured her mother, giving her a hug. By now the boys had managed to get all the way down the stairs and everybody seemed to be hugging everybody else. This is what the TV adverts would call "A Kodak moment" but then you never have a camera when you really need it, do you?

Bit by bit the full story came to light. An advertisement had been placed in a number of gay contact magazines with the Cobbler's address as the return point. For a month or so a steady trickle of letters dropped through the door offering a variety of interesting sado-masochistic scenarios, both homo- and heterosexual, for re-enactment but when no replies were forthcoming the trickle slowed and eventually stopped altogether. The identity of the person placing the advert was never discovered and the whole incident faded into the general background of allegations and counter-allegations. However, we all know of a gentleman who used to be a head teacher and who is most certainly into schoolroom type sado-masochism, don't we?

One day it will all come out in spite of the lawyers and their libel threats, this I promise you on my word of honour. The children of Durham City deserve that, if nothing else.

Chapter 3
…….. and Rock 'n' Roll

This chapter is about a man who makes a best-selling CD and TV documentary, then survives an attempt by a paid thug to break both his legs with a baseball bat. It's a funny old world at times, isn't it?

The problem is that as soon as you start reading about somebody attempting to break somebody else's legs with a baseball bat, the average person's mind simply starts wandering off into the wrong place. Violence comes in two sorts, real-life violence and fictional violence. Thankfully most people only experience fictional violence, and in the world of fictional violence anything can happen. Every day people are riddled with Uzi bullets, blown to pieces, have the blood sucked out of them by giant insect-like aliens on space stations. By those standards having both your legs broken with a baseball bat is quite tame.

Now get your mind back into the real world. Most people's real life experience of violence is very limited, a harsh word may be exchanged, and people stop talking to each other, neighbours glare at each other over fences. All of this is a million miles away from a situation where somebody hates you so much that they are willing to close your business down by paying somebody £200 to injure you so much that you will be unable to work for several months.

Try to place yourself in this situation for just a moment, and if that does not scare you enough, add in a further complication where you know that if the assassin succeeds his crime will not be investigated because the authorities will not allow it to be investigated. A nightmare? No - part of their everyday working lives for Tony Martin and his father at this time.

The most senior members of Durham City Council believed that drastic action was needed, because the situation was becoming desperate. They had tried to brand the Cobbler as a drug-dealer, and it had backfired badly. The Cobbler's window was testimony to new and various stories of corruption and sleaze, as the lid on Durham Labour Party and City Council gradually opened and the dirt seeped out. They were becoming the laughing stock of Durham City, and the Regional Labour Party did not like it at all. Labour Chief Whip Hilary Armstrong had threatened to suspend City of Durham Constituency Labour Party at the National Conference in 1996, but was dissuaded from doing so because of the bad publicity. Things had now gone from bad to worse, Private Eye had christened Durham City "The Rottenest Borough in England" and it was time for the Labour Party to read the Riot Act.

Chris Lennie (later to be promoted to Assistant General Secretary to the Labour Party and given responsibility for the disciplinary action against Glasgow MP George Galloway) was chosen to do the reading along with another gentleman from Labour North, Brian Thistlethwaite. A preliminary meeting of the most important City Council members took place behind closed doors, followed by a second meeting with members of the local Constituency Labour Party. The Riot Act reading sounded something like this:

"No, we will not root out corruption and give our enemies an opportunity to laud it over us, we will put it all behind us, forget about it and pull together for victory. In the past it has been the perception of the national Labour Party that the City of Durham is the most corrupt in England. That must change, and you are the ones who can change it, not us. Forget the Cobbler, he will go away soon. On the way out please collect your forms to recruit more Labour Party members, because quantity rather than quality is what we need at this time. Tony needs their votes and your credit card number. Thank you and goodnight"

Within a few months of this meeting there was a big dispute at Labour North about the way that allegations of corruption within the party were being handled. Brian Thistlethwaite left, leaving Chris Lennie in charge. From that time on, all allegations of corruption within the party were referred to him, and his tactic was to refuse to investigate them. He became the Invisible Man of Labour North, the one you needed to talk to and the one who was never there. This must have been a shrewd career move because in 2003 he was promoted to the post of Assistant General Secretary of the National Labour Party, with David Triesman as General Secretary. Yes, cream rises to the top, but so does all sorts of other floaty things that I have been warned I cannot mention for fear of legal action.

Meanwhile, across the road from Durham Labour Club the Cobbler had been busy. You could not see through his window for press cuttings. New Statesman, Private Eye and national press were all publishing the information brought into his shop by dissatisfied Durham citizens, and he put them into his window. The Council's solicitor dug up a law dating back to 1361, which was all about incitement to a breach of the peace, and claimed that the Cobbler and his window amounted to this. The first the Cobbler knew about it was a phone call from Peter McCusker of the Journal, asking whether he knew a file had been sent to the Crown Prosecution

Service. The Cobbler demanded to know who had made the complaint, but never found out.

A letter also arrived from Thompson's Solicitors who were acting for the Usual Suspects -John Bowman, Maurice Crathorne and Mildred Brown, saying that if offending posters were not removed from the Cobbler's window legal action would be taken against him, and that Mr Laffey from Thompsons would be out to inspect the window to see if the material had gone. The Cobbler was having none of it and put the solicitor's letter next to the picture of Crathorne sunning himself at Durham Miner's Gala. The solicitor did arrive the following Monday to check the window, but did not stay long after the Cobbler threatened to make a citizen's arrest for parking illegally outside his shop. No legal action followed, but a substantial bill from Thompson Solicitors did. Just who paid this bill remains a mystery to this day, but it was either Council Tax money or Labour Party funds.

By now the infamous Cobbler's window was about as full as it could get, and it was time to branch out into multimedia, Tony thought. That is how The Cobbler's CD, The Cobbler's Website and The Cobbler's TV Documentary came about. Looking back it was probably The Cobbler's Website that caused the most anguish to the councillors, because just like the Neanderthal's fear of fire you are most afraid of the things you know least about. Your average councillor knew something about CDs and TVs, but computers and the internet were all part of a completely unknown and frightening world.

The CD, Tony's version of Roger Whittaker's "Durham Town" with a few bits changed to make it more topical, sold out in its first pressing almost immediately. A copy reached Roger Whittaker's record company BMG who owned the copyright of the song and a phone call warning that Durham City Council was about to take legal action against the Cobbler soon persuaded the record company that it was not in their interest to be associated with that sort of thing and copyright was refused, despite the fact that the Cobbler's version was outselling the original. Legal action was threatened, and so ended a promising career in the music business. It is interesting to note that the Cobbler first performed this song in Durham Masonic Hall (at a strictly non-masonic function I have been urged to point out!), but since everybody says that the Freemasons run Durham City and you have a much better chance of living a long and happy life if you do not mention them, it is probably best to draw a veil over that particular episode. We have been taught to be cautious, as the saying goes.

Meanwhile in cyberspace <http://www.cobblers2thecouncil.com> was born, and the councillors who had failed in their legal action turned to illegal action. The first signs that something was about to happen took place when The Cobbler noticed a senior citizen who often came to his shop window to peer between the gaps in the press cuttings to see if there were any customers in the shop. If there was nobody in, she would come and talk about her concerns for his safety. Was he not afraid that if he kept on doing this sort of thing he might get into trouble? One day the truth came out.

"If you put that stuff on the internet, you'll get your legs broke" she screeched.

"What did you say?" questioned the Cobbler, not quite believing what he had heard the first time.

"If you put that stuff on the internet, you'll get your legs broke" she screeched again.

"Do you see that up there?" Tony said, pointing to an insect destroyer. "It's a camera and microphone. What you have just said is now on tape."

The effect was instant and devastating. The senior citizen started yelping and scurried around the shop in circles, as if looking for the door but unable to find it in her anguish. Tony could not help thinking about the time when a sparrow got into his living room, because it was the same sort of feeling. You did not want it to damage any of your ornaments with its wings, but also you did not want it to hurt itself in its panic.

"Who told you to say that?" Tony demanded.

"I'm sorry, I'm sorry, I didn't mean it, honestly….." She found the door handle and escaped from the shop. She was halfway down the street when the Cobbler caught up with her. The City Council CCTV cameras, perched high on the Council offices and a member of the public called Phillip Smith witnessed the Cobbler pursuing the hapless pensioner down the street.

"Excuse me, could you be a witness to this?" said the Cobbler to the wide-eyed passer-by. "This woman has just come into my shop and threatened that I will have my legs broken if I put the stuff in my window onto the internet. She has also admitted that Durham City Council had sent her in with the threats"

"Me heart, me heart, me heart!" the old lady shrieked. Worried that she might fall down dead in the street, the pair backed off and she calmed down slightly. Bit by bit the story came out and the astonished passer by became even more astonished as the story of the threats unfolded. By now the cameras were pointing at the scene and the Cobbler waved at them, sure that the whole incident had been captured.

"Will you be a witness to this, Mr Smith?" the Cobbler asked.

"I certainly will. This is unbelievable. Is this the sort of thing you have to put up with all the time?" he asked.

"Yes, it is and I'm sick of it." the Cobbler replied.

The police were called in but the incident was referred to one of The Usual Suspects, Superintendent Suddes. As you will see later, this gentleman always seems to arrive, like the cavalry over the hill, when one of our councillors is in trouble. Sure enough, several weeks later the Cobbler was told that nothing had been caught on CCTV. In fact despite the fact that the woman had walked past dozens of CCTV cameras on her way back to North Road she had managed to evade every single camera, a feat that thousands of motorists would envy. She was not quite so lucky, however when a year later the Cobbler, lunch in hand, caught her coming out of the charity shop just down the road. As she fled, another passer-by identified her as Nell Gibbon. Anyone know a Nell Gibbon?

In real life threats of violence are bound to make you wary, even when they come from an unlikely source such as a frightened senior citizen. She must have had some good reason to be as frightened as that, Tony thought. It might have been this that made him cautious or it could be that there is really such a thing as a sixth sense warning you about imminent danger, because Tony knew that something was going to happen. He sensed it even more strongly one night a few weeks later as he closed his shop for the night and headed alone up the narrow alley beside his shop.

Remember once again that we are talking about real-life violence here. If you have never been involved in real-life violence there are a few things you have got to understand. First and foremost, real-life violence happens much, much faster than TV violence. Things happen in a fraction of a second and one person is standing up and somebody else is on the floor. Things are never as tidy as on TV, because in that instant of violence things can happen which are beyond the control of the people who are involved. Once the blood is up anything can happen, ranging from people losing their dignity to people losing their lives. It is all the luck of the game because when you are really afraid the animal instinct to survive takes over and the body does what is necessary without the brain having a great deal to do with it. Most fights consist of only one punch.

Secondly, real life violence is about ten times messier than anything you can see on movies or TV. A man who has been punched hard in the face will fall to the floor with his face covered in the blood spurting from a flattened nose. He will spit blood and broken teeth and he may vomit as he lies there. This is far scarier than watching an animatronic alien insect eating a man, because this is real. You can smell real-life blood, and that is a smell not easily forgotten.

Tony walked around the corner and without seeing him he knew that the man with the upraised baseball bat was there. For weeks now the Cobbler had had a feeling in the pit of his stomach that the best solution to all of his problems was to hit somebody hard in the mouth, and all of the pent-up anger went into that single punch. With a surprised look on his face the man fell backwards, but almost before he hit the floor the Cobbler grabbed him by the collar with his right hand and dragged him into the doorway of his shop. In his left hand was the unused baseball bat.

By now the man was inside the shop, lying on the floor and the shop door was locked. A thin rope of saliva and blood trickled from the corner of his mouth.

"Who sent you?" Silence.

"Who....f*cking...sent you?" The words were slow and deliberate. Silence.

Crack ! There was an unmistakable cracking of bone as the baseball bat impacted on the man's kneecap. Both hands shot to the knee and stayed there. The mouth was wide open in pain, white teeth covered in red.

"It was Bowman, John Bowman! He paid me £200 to break your legs so you couldn't work. Honest!"

"Well tell Bowman I'm going to break his f*cking legs the next time I see him. Now f*ck off out of my shop and don't come back. Or else." The door was unlocked and the man was outside in the street, hobbling away as quickly as he could.

You would have thought that if two men were involved in a fight like this and one man gets a broken kneecap they would be bitter enemies for the rest of their lives. Funnily enough, it did not work out like that. In fact, later the hit-man returned to the shop to apologise. He had been offered £200 and he really needed money at the time. His kneecap had only been cracked, had healed quickly but his jaw was still wired up. The councillor who had hired him remained in a senior position on Durham City Council until the electoral bloodbath of May 2003. There were no further attempts at violence but the threats continued.

As I said at the start of this chapter, it's a funny old world at times, isn't it?

Chapter 4
A Black Cloud Looms

From hell's heart I stab at thee! I spit my last breath at thee, for hate's sake!

Herman Melville

That quote was from the book Moby Dick, and I'm sure you have either read the book or seen the film with Gregory Peck as Captain Ahab. These are the last words of Captain Ahab who is tied to his lifelong enemy, a big white whale, and cursing it as he stabs at it with a big harpoon. He knows that he is tied up with something a lot bigger than he is, and in a minute it is going to drag him down to destruction, but in the meantime he is going to get just a little bit of pay-back. This book is the Cobbler's harpoon, and it's time to get on with the stabbing.

Harsh language has changed a great deal since Herman Melville's time and this chapter contains quite a lot of it, so please do not continue to read this chapter if you are offended by that sort of thing. Hey, you - are you still here? I thought I just told you to f*ck off, didn't I? Go on, f*ck off and read something else, you great soft sh*te. What - you're still here? Listen carefully; I'll spell it out for you.   F - * - C- K   O- F _-F   -   NOW!   Go on.......just f*ck off! ......Right, that's got rid of all the soft c*nts. Now we can get on with telling the story.

The power of words to hurt people is amazing. Teachers have known this for a long time of course, and I am sure the oldies amongst us can remember teachers whose tongues hurt almost as much as their canes. When children complain about bullying in the playground, most of the time they are talking not of actual physical violence (which does take place of course) but simply incessant name-calling. When this goes on day after day, week after week and there is no end to it, eventually the victim's spirit is destroyed completely and it is little wonder that sometimes it all ends in a suicide attempt. The real difference between man and the animals is our power to communicate through words, and if you abuse that you are abusing our most precious faculty. *(Oh, f*ck - I think I'm having an attack of philosophy.)*

If you take words and write them down on paper or distribute them via television to millions of people, you have an immensely powerful tool for good or evil. I am telling you nothing new of course, because people were saying that the pen is

36

mightier than the sword when the pen was made out of a bird's feather. Has this changed in the twenty-first century? The pen may be mightier than the sword but is it mightier than the AK-47? Is it mightier than a fleet of bombers dropping fire on helpless Vietnamese children? Is it mightier than hundreds of intercontinental ballistic missiles with nuclear warheads that can destroy humanity at the touch of a button? Discuss. I want a five thousand-word essay on my desk by Monday morning, please. Now f*ck off.

A lot of new political thinking took place in both large political parties in the last quarter of the twentieth century, and the result changed the face of Britain. Up until the time of Margaret Thatcher, politicians fought for every single vote, but The Iron Lady changed all of that. She reasoned that there are certain people - low-income families, trade unionists for example - who will *never* vote for you, no matter what you do to them. That meant there was no point in chasing their vote, you could ignore them, even make life difficult for them as an example to others. And she did. The ones you really needed to keep on your side were the opinion-makers like Rupert Murdoch.

This technique worked well, and the Labour Party took notice of it during the eighteen-year reign of Thatcherism. When Tony Blair came to power in 1997, he took the philosophy one step further. He reasoned that there are certain people - low-income families, trade unionists for example - who will *always* vote for you, no matter what you do to them. That meant there was no point in chasing their vote, you could ignore them, even make life difficult for them as an example to others. And he did. The ones you really needed to keep on your side were the opinion-makers like Rupert Murdoch.

Tony took this philosophy even further than Thatcher however. Traditionally politicians have employed thousands of civil servants to try to make things go smoothly in the country, because if you did not, then all your cock-ups got into the newspapers and this damaged the credibility of the government. A shrewd bit of thinking by Alderman Blair's little lad came to the devastatingly simple conclusion that it did not really matter what sort of cock-ups went on in the country, as long as it did not get into the newspapers or on television. If you could not prevent it getting into the newspapers, then twist the facts until they fit what you want to say. A palatable lie is better than an unpalatable truth, the reasoning goes - Richard Nixon's doctrine of Plausible Deniability all over again.

Bit by bit the emphasis changed from getting the country to run smoothly to making it look as if the country was running smoothly in the newspapers and on television.

Spin-doctors like Peter Mandelson and Alistair Campbell became the backroom boys who ran the country, both of them becoming notoriously unpleasant bullies as they wielded the power of their master, Tony Blair. All that was needed were the two magic words "Tony wants…." and people snapped to attention.

Anyone not snapping to attention soon found themselves spending much more time with their families because there were a lot of staffing changes to be made, since now you only needed a few people keeping an eye on the newspapers and television rather than a lot of people keeping an eye on every aspect of the workings of the country. The Hutton Report gave the public some idea of how the notoriously foul-mouthed bullying spin-doctors at the heart of the New Labour revolution might have managed a ministerial downsizing operation like this. Imagine a scene in an office in the Ministry of Doublespeak at Walworth Road. The Minister picks up his telephone.

"Hello, look Tony wants some changes. We need to lose more people. Slim down the departments, cut out the dead wood, revitalise growth, that sort of thing, you know…….Yeh, well I'm sorry for them but like they say, sh*t happens. That's what they're in the pension scheme for……. What do you mean, they're not in the pension scheme…….What, Margaret Thatcher's personal advice?.........Serves the stupid c*nts right for listening to her.........I couldn't give a f*ck if she was Prime Minister, it wasn't my fault, I didn't vote for her…… No.........Look, f*ck Margaret Thatcher….Oh, my god, what have I said……..No, I don't think even Tony would do that…..god, no - not even if she took her false teeth out - you just cannot trust that bitch……….Yeh, look, I'm sorry but we're wasting time here, they're going to have to go……What do you mean who…..yes, all of them. We are switching resources into the media departments. ……Yes, education, all of them have got to go. We don't need anybody keeping an eye on the f*cking teachers…….yes, health service as well, anybody who is anybody is in BUPA……good way to keep the waiting lists down, let all the benefits leeches die off…….Yes, police as well, we don't need anybody keeping an eye on the coppers……What do you mean, they've all gone already…….When?…….How many years?…….F*ck me…So who is supposed to have been keeping the coppers in line all these years, the guy in charge must be blind not to realise……..Oh, my god, of course, ha ha………Well that was Tony's idea, some sort of quota, I think……Yes, even in the cabinet….I agree, a total waste of f*cking space, worth his weight in fish heads, but it looks good on TV now we haven't got any ethnic minorities in the cabinet…..You know, cripples, blackies, fudge-packers, that sort of thing……..no, Peter's not in the cabinet any more…Anyway, you don't seem to be much f*cking use, you don't know what an ethnic minority is, you're supposed

38

to be keeping me in the loop and you haven't told me that the coppers have been a law unto themselves for twenty years.......Look, I'll use that f*cking tone of voice to anybody I want, I am Director of Communications for the Labour Party, and I'm telling you that in three month's time you're out of a job, it's as simple as that.........No, f*ck you, you're sacked, which bit of that don't you understand?........golden handshake, what do you mean, golden f*cking handshake, who do you think you are, John f*cking Prescott?.........Oh, sorry, John, I didn't recognise you there, are you on your mobile?.....Look, catch you later, OK John, cheers"

Puts down the phone.

This is all very well, but what has it got to do with corruption in Durham City, and what's all this about a black cloud? What you have to remember is that bullying is not just restricted to the school playground, it can also happen in adult life. Political leaders like Blair and Thatcher pride themselves on their strong leadership, but how do the people feel about being led strongly? "A manager's job is to manage," said Margaret Thatcher. Up and down the country leaders of industry latched onto the hidden agenda of this statement and took this as a clear indication that Britain was meant to be a country where a boss was bossy and a worker just worked. A whole new era of workplace bullying began.

There were still a few honest men and women prepared to stand up for what they believed in and one of these was Council Leader Bill Kellett. There had been friction between Bill Kellett, John Bowman and Maurice Crathorne before, relating to the theft of drinks from the City Council drinks cabinet. Bill Kellett had called in the police after Crathorne and Bowman had broken into the cabinet in Kellett's office a number of times. In spite of a great deal of evidence, the police did not bring charges. They accepted Crathorne's explanation that he was "Only helping the lads to a drink." Several hundred drinks, actually.

When it came around to the time for the election of a new council leader, the choice was between Kellett and Crathorne. Kellett's electoral platform was simple and straightforward. "Elect me and I will rid Durham City Council of corruption." Crathorne's approach was quite different, but can be summarised as "Here's a pint, lad. Vote for me and I'll put a few quid in your back pocket." Of course, Crathorne won easily, because nobody fails by underestimating the honesty of the average Labour Durham City councillor and the scene was now set for a new era of underhand dealings.

Not everything was going to plan, however. There was a black cloud hanging over Durham City Council in the form of a gentleman named Abadun McWilliams, and it was hanging blackest of all over the head of Durham City's blondest ex-mayor, Mildred Brown. "The Black Bastard" was Mildred's nickname for Abadun McWilliams, because as well as being Health and Safety Officer for Durham City Council and Chairman of Durham City Magistrates, Mac (as he was known to his many friends) was a gentleman of colour. "The Black Cloud" and "The Blacky up at Byeland Lodge" and "Black Mac" were just a few of the taunts that Mac had to put up with on a daily basis.

Of course there is always a certain amount of horseplay and banter in any office environment, and the offices of Durham City Council were no exception. There have to be limits of course, and there was the matter of the Racial Discrimination Act. By now I hope that you have come to realise that abiding by the law of the land was not always a high priority within Durham City Council. Neither was respect for the feelings of the workforce, and when people kept on greeting Mac with "Hello, you black bastard " when it was obvious that the joke had worn thin, trouble was on the way.

In order to understand The McWilliams Allegations, as they came to be known, you must first understand the mindset of Durham councillors prior to 1st May 2003. Until that time they regarded themselves as impregnable. Gerry Steinberg MP was immensely proud of his majority. "We don't count the Labour votes in Durham, we weigh them." Others were less complimentary. "If a monkey stood for Labour in Durham, it would get elected, " is another comment I remember well. Since the Local Government reorganisation in 1974 the district of Durham had been a solid Labour fiefdom. Most people could never remember a time when Durham had been anything other than brick red Labour through and through.

Most people know Lord Acton's quotation about "Power corrupts. Absolute power corrupts absolutely". Now Crathorne and Co. did not quite possess absolute power, but they thought they did. With that thought came arrogance and a total disregard for anyone who disagreed with them. Power of this sort is dangerous and it takes a special sort of person to wield it without being corrupted. Sadly for Labour they were not always as careful in choosing their candidates as they should have been and eventually the democratic process became an irrelevance, because once you got the Labour nomination, you were home and dry. The election became little more than a formality and once elected, you could do more or less whatever you wanted and get elected over and over again. It did not matter if you were wrinkled, paunchy and signed your name with a big "X." You were the top predator and Durham City was your jungle. You could afford to be utterly contemptuous of the feelings and aspirations of Council employees, and indeed many councillors were. They knew that if the employees complained they would be complaining about councillors to councillors. One phone call and even their trade union support was gone. Solicitors, courts of law, judges - don't even think about it. One word over the Festive Board and that sort of thing became the equivalent of making a bonfire of your life savings. Some employees got out but most just got used to it, ignored it and got on with the job. Not Abadun McWilliams.

To be fair to Mildred she was not only one who made fun of Mac's skin colour. In fact she was not even the one who irritated him the most. The most persistent and offensive irritant was a man called David Marrs. Mac could tolerate the light-hearted references to "The blackie at Byland Lodge" or "How are you today, you black b*stard?" as long as it was said with a smile on the face and an arm around the shoulder. David Marrs was openly contemptuous of Mac and everything that he did, and that hurt far more than thoughtless references to the colour of his skin.

As Health & Safety Officer to the Council, Mac's responsibilities were widespread. As well as more mundane tasks such as making sure that scaffolding was safe to work upon, he had quite a lot to do with the emotional welfare of the City Council's workforce. When Senior Recreation Officer Alan Wilson punched his deputy, Keith Walton, in the face during a heated argument at an international cross-country meeting in March 1995, Mac poured the oil on the troubled waters that seemed likely to submerge Alan Wilson's career. The trauma of two ladies discovering a murder victim was also passed on to him, and he dealt with it in a way that won him the respect of the people around. All except for David Marrs, who felt that Mac was sticking his dark-coloured nose into areas where it did not belong, and told him so in unmistakable terms.

A Durham City Council scandal would not be complete without Colin Shearsmith, and this one is no exception. Twelve years of taunting and abusive racist remarks came to a head in a dispute with David Marrs over the accommodation of a female Welfare & Safety officer. David Marrs lost his temper with Mac and stormed out of the room threatening to "put her into a cupboard and throw away the key." instead of giving her an office as Mac had asked.

Almost at the end of his tether by now Mac went to Colin Shearsmith as Marrs' line-manager. Mr Shearsmith was a blunt man at times, not above calling a spade a "meddling black b*stard" himself, and his comment of "David Marrs is a nice lad, I appointed him" sums up the meeting nicely. He mentioned the incident to Marrs, but the pair of them were openly dismissive of "the blackie and his trade union buddies," and from then on Colin Shearsmith simply ignored Mac's complaints.

Eventually the situation deteriorated to the point where Mac felt so uncomfortable about even being in the same room as Marrs that something had to be done. If you have never been in a workplace situation that has deteriorated into "hell with fluorescent lighting" as one ex-council employee described it, then think yourself lucky. Most of us spend more hours in paid employment than anywhere else during our adult lives, and to have that turned into a situation that wrenches your stomach as you put the car-keys into the lock on a weekday morning is not a happy state of affairs. Mac did the only thing he could, and brought the whole sad situation to the attention of his trade union. Let's digress a moment and talk a little bit about trade unionism in Durham.

Once upon a time Durham City was the pride and joy of the trade union movement. Every year there was the showpiece Miners Gala, and no respectable leader of the Labour Party would dare miss the opportunity to address the tens of thousands of miners and other workers who would stream through the city, following the colourful banners and strident brass bands as they marched to the old Racecourse next to the River Wear to "get their rights."

My grandfather was different. Every year of his adult life on Big Meeting Day he took the Gypsy Queen bus service from Langley Park to Durham, but never got closer to the celebrations than the Garden House pub outside County Hall where he celebrated until blissful unconsciousness overtook him and somebody put him onto a Gypsy Queen bus headed for home.

Those were the good old days of trade unionism, but this is 1997. Margaret Thatcher's laws weakened the power of the unions, but New Labour corruption destroyed it completely. "No industrial action - wait until we get into power" turned to "No industrial action - wait until we get the second term" Although the leaders of the big trades unions were no longer invited through the front door of No. 10 Downing Street for beer and sandwiches, the New Labour revolution was being planned on the backs of beer-mats at £300-per-head Indian restaurants, and being a spectator was much better than being outside in the cold. For the ordinary worker the roles of boss, enemy and friend were now hopelessly confused and you could not be sure just who your union rep was representing any more.

Fortunately for Mac he had a friend in John Turnbull, one of the old style union reps. UCATT Convenor Turnbull had crossed swords with David Marrs on a number of occasions, and had little time for the man

"I do not want to pursue this case because it will damage my relationship with Durham City Council" said Mac's union rep, as he tried to bury the case. Mac was having none of it and persisted. As more and more witness statements mounted up, Unison realised that they would be forced to do something about it and Mildred Brown became desperate. There was only one person who could help her now and that was Joe Anderson. Joe had been in the Labour Party for a long time and had amassed a tremendous amount of local info during his time as Mayor. If anybody could help he could, because he knew where all the bodies were buried. Unfortunately Mildred made a big mistake, because instead of asking Joe to do her a favour as he had done for so many people before, she tried to blackmail him.

Joe still had his Wellingtons on from digging in his allotment when the doorbell rang. Joe went to the door and opened it. Outside was Mildred with an unmistakably triumphant look in her eye. Trouble for somebody, thought Joe.

"Come on in lass, what can I do for you?"

"Look Joe, I've got something to show you" Mildred said, thrusting a letter into his hand. Joe looked at it for a moment, then looked up at Mildred in astonishment.

"Where did you get that from?" Joe asked, passing the letter back to her. "The police told me they had destroyed it"

The cause of Joe's astonishment, the letter Mildred had given him, was a letter that had surfaced about twelve months before accusing Joe and two other councillors of being involved in a paedophile ring. It had gone to the police who had investigated it, and found it to be a completely false accusation. Joe had been told that the letter had been destroyed and no further action was to be taken. It had gone through two sets of hands, Colin Shearsmith and Maurice Crathorne . Nobody had said anything about copying it before it had gone to the police though. Joe suddenly understood that a copy of this vital letter had been made, and there could only be one reason why this should have been done. Blackmailing him into silence.

"Now listen Joe, Mac is making these allegations of racial abuse against me and David. You can stop him, I know. Now the thing is, if you don't stop him, this letter goes to the newspapers and I've got friends in the newspapers, you know that." Mildred's eyes betrayed the intensity of her feelings. "I warn you, if I go down I'm taking everybody with me."

Joe exploded with anger. "You can do whatever you bloody want, but get out of my house first and never come back again. You know that that letter is a complete lie, and if you try to publish it you will regret it. Now get out."

Mildred was completely taken aback by this and left in a great hurry. A great deal of telephoning took place in the next few hours. Joe to police, police to other police, police to Mildred and Mildred to lots and lots of people, none of who could help her out of the big black hole that was getting deeper and blacker by the minute. Now instead of just facing charges of racial abuse she had just added blackmail to the charge sheet, and Joe Anderson wanted her expulsion from the Labour Party. Meanwhile Mac's racial abuse case was going ahead.

In spite of the fact that the police had allegedly sent a file to the Crown Prosecution Service the only notification that Joe ever received was a phone call from Usual Suspect Superintendent Suddes, telling him that there was insufficient evidence for a prosecution to go ahead, even though she had admitted going to his house with the letter. It took years of letter writing until December 2003 when the Cobbler and Joe Anderson made a joint complaint about Jeff Corrigan, Head of Durham Crown Prosecution Service to Richard Foster, Head of CPS Complaints Department, who filed the complaints without response to Joe's letter, and fobbed the Cobbler off with a pack of lies.

Meanwhile back to the plot - Mac's union, Unison, were still threatening to bring his case to an employment tribunal but behind the scenes they were pressurising him to settle out of court. One by one Mac's witnesses dropped out after alleged threats from Maurice Crathorne. Eventually Mac was forced to settle for a sum of about £6,500, much less than he deserved. The meeting of City of Durham Constituency Labour Party that reported the settlement was one of the most eventful I can ever remember, and it was also the first time that most Labour Party members got to hear about the activities of the soon-to-be-infamous Durham Cobbler.

If there was a black cloud hanging over Mildred Brown, then Colin Shearsmith had his own personal thunderstorm going on around him, and try as he might Gerry Steinberg MP could not keep a lid on the whole thing any more. Generally speaking the last-Saturday-in-the-month constituency meetings were fairly routine with all the potential problems being ironed out at the executive meetings the Wednesday evening beforehand. Not so this time, because as well as Mildred's Mishap there was the dreadful business of the Ransom Strip to be considered. These two biggies promised to provide the delegates with entertainment the like of which they had never seen before.

I have absolutely no qualifications as a Town Planner and therefore my understanding of the Ransom Strip incident is probably so simplistic as to be unrepresentative of the truth, but here it is. Most people buy a piece of land and then build on it because this is the accepted wisdom. To build your house first and then ask to buy the land afterwards is just a little bit arse-before-tit, as the expression goes. Nevertheless that is essentially what the officers of Durham City Council did, and now they were going to have to explain why to the delegates of City of Durham CLP. That is a simplification of course, because they bought most of the land and started work before somebody pointed out that "due to circumstances beyond our control (disclaimer, disclaimer) we should have bought this little bit of land, but seem to have forgotten to do so. Now the owner realises that if we don't buy this piece of land from him we are well & truly rubber-ducked, and he is asking us to pay a large sum of council-taxpayers money for it".

"It's called a Ransom Strip in the trade" Mr Steinberg assured us. "It's not very nice, but it's normal business practice, I'm afraid. In fact, the City Council have done the same thing themselves in the past" Well, that's all right then, we breathed a sigh of relief. The alternative hypothesis was that the Council was staffed by fools and criminals, a truly frightening prospect indeed. We were all so pleased that our MP could provide the reassurance that this was not the case. "Nevertheless," Mr Steinberg continued "it is important that the Cobbler doesn't get to know about it."

The guy who wrote the story of The Emperor's New Clothes would have been convulsed with laughter if he had been there because almost everybody was thinking to themselves "What's a cobbler got to do with a City Council land deal?" but since it was not considered cool to be seen to be out of the loop, information-wise, they all simply kept quiet and savoured the prospect of the day's main entertainment, which was to be Mildred Brown's apology to Mr McWilliams. This took place during Maurice Crathorne's City Council report.

"I'm so sorry Mac," said Mildred, gaunt and close to tears. "It was just a joke. We were just trying to have a bit of fun. You know we wouldn't do anything to hurt you, pet." There was a strange low-level sound that I could not place at the time, but in retrospect it was almost certainly the sound of one hundred sets of middle-aged teeth being set into full grit by the sound of this cringe-making apology for an apology.

"I'll talk to the delegate myself in private after the meeting" Mac replied simply, and sat down. One hundred delegates prayed to be converted into flies on the flock-wallpapered walls of the Labour club for long enough to hear that conversation, but to my knowledge none of their prayers were granted and the subsequent conversation remained confidential. Maurice Crathorne stood up to resume his report.

"It's important that we put this episode behind us and above all we have got to make sure the Cobbler doesn't get to know about it." Once again, the mysterious cobbler is mentioned.

"Where's he getting his information from?" one delegate asked.

"I know. There's a nigger in the woodpile, and I know who that nigger is!" Crathorne pointed accusingly across the room.

"You can't say that sort of thing any more, Maurice" Mildred pleaded, pulling his sleeve, but Maurice had the bit between his teeth and was not about to be diverted.

" I accuse……." Crathorne paused momentarily to increase the dramatic effect of his revelation "….Bill Kellett!" he shouted triumphantly, pointing across to the corner where his predecessor as leader of Durham City Council sat. All eyes swivelled in the direction of his gnarled finger, searching for the aforesaid nigger. Bill Kellett, sunburnt from hours in his garden but definitely non-negroid, appeared to shrink slightly as if trying to merge with the background. Exhausted with all this unusual excitement I left the room and went downstairs for a drink in the bar, passing Mac and Mildred who seemed to be too deep in conversation to notice.

Looking down and along the street to the Cobbler's shop I noticed a crowd of people standing outside the shop, pointing at the window in an animated fashion. In the window was a small collection of articles cut from local newspapers and highlighted with black felt-tipped pen. As I was to find out later, the information in the Cobbler's window represented a fuller and more accurate picture of what was going on in Durham City than anything that was presented to the executive members of City of Durham Constituency Labour Party. I finished my drink and went back into the meeting, just in time to hear Pat Nolan appealing on behalf of fellow County Councillor Ron Morrissey.

"What are we going to do about Ron Morrissey?" Pat pleaded "It's not fair on the man to be suspended all this length of time" Pat made no mention of the fact that Ron himself had very little concern about fairness. It was obvious to everybody in the room that the Labour Party were simply playing for time until his period of office as a County Councillor expired, which meant that they did not have to take

46

any disciplinary action against him with all the damaging publicity that would bring in its wake.

Ron had been Gerry Steinberg's electoral agent, Chairman of the Education Committee of Durham County Council, Vice-Chair of the Finance & Property Committee as well as chairing various other governing bodies and committees until one of the biggest scandals in recent local Labour Party history overtook him. The governing bodies of the schools, hospitals and various charitable organisations within the county were the favourite playgrounds of councillors who wished to exercise power and authority over others, and to sweeten it all there was even the opportunity to make a few quid on the side if you knew where to look, and Ron most certainly knew where to look.

Secure in his power and position, Ron would saunter through the schools where he held power, often stopping to reprimand a teacher in front of his class if he was displeased with what he saw. Even the dreaded OFSTED inspectors would not dare to do that, but Ron was not the sort of man to pussyfoot around, as he was very keen to tell everyone. Bit by bit a scandal started to leak out that was so big even the devious Durham County Council solicitors could not keep it hidden from Senior Charity Commissioner Alan Martin, who in his report questioned the wisdom of the closed-door cabinet decision making that had allowed all of this to happen.

Allegedly Morrissey had been using his power as chairman of various organisations, especially a training agency called Interchurch and Christ's Hospital at Sherburn, to siphon off money and benefits into his own pocket over a period of twelve years. In addition it was alleged that he had paid himself a generous pension and had diverted other money into an investment in Spain that had gone adrift. To add to the scandal a local vicar, Graham Pattison, was implicated and later had his licence to preach revoked by the Church of England and a number of other Labour Councillors were also on the fringes of the scandal.

The exact size of the financial misdemeanour will never be known because the Durham County Council solicitors worked as hard as they could in their damage limitation exercise. Ron was never charged with anything, but eventually he was required to pay back about £40,000. Rev Patterson was forced to repay over £100, 000 and was removed from the Church. Fellow Sherburn Labour Party member John Bowman, himself not averse to earning a few quid from his governing body activities as you will see later, aided and abetted him and suffered the indignity of a mild slap on the wrist as a consequence.

When public pressure forced Ron to resign from his school governing bodies, other Sherburn Labour Party members moved in to fill the gap. Ray Pye, John Bowman's brother-in-law took over chairmanship of Ron's favourite school, Belmont Comprehensive School, and eventually his position as County Councillor for Sherburn. The staff of Belmont Comp who had hoped for a change of management style as well as a change of management were soon disappointed. Some disastrous management appointments that appeared to have been engineered in the smoke-filled back rooms of County Hall left the school on the brink of chaos and OFSTED Special Measures.

Violence and bullying were rife in the school and assaults on staff commonplace. Ex-County rugby player and referee Fred Lowes, who was Head of PE, was beaten up in the changing rooms, his injuries forced him to retire and he died ten years later without recovering his health. Christine Walker-Jones was punched in the back and the injuries to her spine forced her into retirement. She was on a temporary contract and the governing body simply terminated it, denying that the assault had ever taken place. Enraged by the fact that she had been denied compensation unfairly Mrs Walker-Jones took her story to the Mail on Sunday, who published it as a double page spread.

The school seemed to be permanently short of money, in complete contrast to the neighbouring Gilesgate Comprehensive chaired by the fiercely independent Dennis Southwell, who eventually resigned from the Labour Party in disgust and now forms part of the LibDem City Council cabinet. In spite of taking a high proportion of their pupils from the notorious Sherburn Road Estate, Gilesgate Comp forged ahead and eventually became the first school in the area to gain Specialist Sports School status. Meanwhile the governors of Belmont Comp, including The Usual Suspects John Bowman, City Council Deputy Leader Steve Laverick and Joe Knight, attempted to save money by manipulating a series of staff redundancies.

One of the teacher trade unions, the NASUWT, took the governing body to an employment tribunal on behalf of one of their members and the tribunal decided that the member of staff in question had been treated unfairly, awarding her several thousands of pounds in compensation. The head teacher, fearing the publicity that was bound to result from that decision, decided that now was a good time to retire. Not so fearless was chairman of governors Ray Pye, who simply decided not to tell anybody that a legal judgement had been made against him.

Helped by the devious legal department of Durham County Council Ray almost got away with it. He managed to cover up the Court's decision for almost six months, by which time he had managed to get himself re-elected as Chairman of the governing body again. His cover was blown at the Autumn school annual general meeting of governors, when awkward questions revealed what had happened. Apparently quite unfazed by the fact that nobody in the room believed his story that a legal judgment had been made against his school six months ago but the solicitors of Durham County Council simply had not got around to telling him, Mr Pye dismissed the whole business. The incoming head teacher, Pat Howarth, ever anxious to back up the man who had just appointed him, uttered the famous line "This sort of thing happens all of the time." Yes, it does Pat, but the question is "Should it happen all the time?"

The story does not end there. The teacher in question was lucky in that she was represented by a relatively honest trade union, the NASUWT. Another member of staff was made redundant under parallel conditions but her union, the National Union of Teachers or NUT, does not appear to have considered that she had a good enough case to take to court. At this present moment Dr Tim Field, who runs the internet's largest anti-workplace bullying website www.bullyonline.org, is being sued by NUT solicitor Graham Clayton for publishing material that suggests that the NUT is not particularly good at representing its teacher members, and that hundreds of teachers have contacted him saying that the NUT has deliberately sabotaged legal cases against their employers It does seem strange that the NUT is very reluctant to take employers to court but when somebody mentions this on an internet website, the NUT takes them to court!

Within Durham politics the Sherburn branch of the Labour Party has had immense influence for many years. So many of the key players in our story, Gerry Steinberg MP, Ron Morrissey, Mildred Brown, John Bowman and his County Council brother-in-law Ray Pye are all from Sherburn, and Colin Shearsmith has strong Sherburn connections. It turns out that Gerry Steinberg MP is a good personal friend of Belmont Comp chair of governors Ray Pye. Ray sponsored Steinberg's nomination as Labour MP candidate at the last election and crucially **Gerry Steinberg is also the parliamentary consultant to the NUT.**

Actually the situation is not quite that simple. The 2002 NUT handbook states quite clearly that Gerry Steinberg MP is their parliamentary consultant. However I have a letter here, which was given to me by an ex-member of staff of Belmont Comp who is complaining about the poor service he also received from the NUT at that school. It was written by Gerry Steinberg MP in 2003, and claims that he has not been an NUT parliamentary consultant for many years now! Come on guys, get your heads together and start telling the same story, at least.

My final comment on this sorry episode has got to be this. If the NUT wins its libel action against Tim Field, I wonder where it will attempt to organise the celebratory piss-up? From what I can see the inside of the Scottish and Newcastle Brewery, right on the doorstep of NUT General Secretary Doug McAvoy, is likely to be a venue that would present insurmountable difficulties for Britain's biggest teacher trade union.

At least that is what I was led to believe until a little bit of research around the subject proved me wrong. The NUT's legal department turns out to be a group of hardworking and capable individuals, but what remains uncertain is whose benefit their talent and effort is directed at. On the face of it a major preoccupation of the legal department of Britain's biggest teaching union seems to be covering up its own mistakes. By senior solicitor Graham Clayton's own admission the Union has been sued by its own members twice, once successfully and once unsuccessfully, and there have been at least two complaints to the Office of Supervision of Solicitors about its legal department. If Tim Field's defence against the NUT is to be believed, recently an Oxfordshire teacher, who was told that she had no prospect of her bullying case succeeding by her NUT lawyer, has just taken it to tribunal herself and won it, despite having no legal training herself and the fact that she is still suffering from psychological injury because of her former employment situation. All in all this looks like being an interesting libel case because if it is proved that the NUT have been sabotaging members' legal cases deliberately as Tim Field alleges, this is likely to be the biggest scandal in trade union history.

This sort of problem is not restricted to the NUT unfortunately. The unions are meant to be the guardians of workers' rights, yet under Labour virtually all workers, apart from Members of Parliament, are working much longer hours than under the Conservatives, and their rights are continuing to be eroded. Why is this? The answer is quite simple. As long as you remember that despite both sides saying that they intend to increase the distance between each other, the Labour Party and the trade union movement are simply different names for the same organisation. Once you get your head around that simple fact then everything becomes plain.

When Labour is in power the trade unions become the most powerful method of regulating the workforce any government could ever wish for. Unison, Britain's biggest trade union is very proud of its Unison - Labour link. It might be good for the Unison officials, and in fact one Unison General Secretary left the union to set up a consultancy hiring nurses back to the NHS at inflated rates of pay, because it earned him more than his £70,000+ union salary. Has it improved the working conditions of the Unison membership, though? The members I have spoken to lead me to believe it has not.

Incidentally, what happened to the Unison Regional secretary who had a legal judgement of workplace bullying made against him? Was he sacked, pensioned off or did it all just blow over? I am dying to find out, and I suspect Mr Abadun McWilliams would like to know as well.

Finally I would have liked to have brought you the story of Avarsi Shah, a young Asian lady who was also subjected to workplace bullying that destroyed her health and career, and who did the rounds of the Durham venues with Mac giving talks about racial discrimination. I attended one of these talks and her presentation was both moving and persuasive. Some time later the Cobbler received a file of documents relating her story labelled "please get justice for this lady."

At the same time there was a gentleman called Chris Close who subscribed to the Cobbler's internet website guest-book under the pseudonym of Enoch Arden, alleging that he was a senior figure within the local NHS looking for hard evidence of local corruption. Give it to him and he would do something about it, he alleged. The file was passed on to him and after several months the Cobbler contacted Mr Close, who alleged that the file had gone to the Unison offices in Newcastle. Even after repeated requests Mr Close has not returned the documentation.

Whether or not the documents did get to Unison or remained with Chris Close we will never know; all we know is that they have disappeared. For further details of how to perform The Disappearing Documentation Trick please read Anatomy of a Stitch-Up at the end of this book. An important part of that trick is to take the advice of Crusty the Clown to children who are in trouble. When all else fails just stand up straight and hold your hands out in front of you, palms open to show you have nothing to hide and say is a loud indignant voice "Don't blame me, *I* didn't do it" placing a strong emphasis on the word "I." Say it over and over again whenever questioned. Believe me, it works remarkably well in a wide variety of awkward situations.

If you are being bullied at work, school or anywhere else, then look for the information about ways of dealing with it on Tim Field's website www.bullyonline.org

Chapter 5
That's Entertainment

You can fool some of the people sometime but you can't fool all of the people all of the time, Now we've seen the light, stand up for your rights.

Bob Marley

Like the early Roman emperors, the kings of Durham City Council were not content with having a steady stream of public money flowing into their personal coffers. Many felt the need to secure for themselves a place in history, something that people will remember them by when they are gone. Bricks and mortar have always been the first choice for a lasting tribute, and Durham City is no exception. Councillors competed with each other to get their names on brass plaques on walls, with all the enthusiasm of little boys collecting Pokemon cards.

The scale of the building depended upon the budget at hand. At the bottom of the scale you had what was laughingly described within the local community as the Belmont Labour Party Memorial Bus Stop, with its view of the wrought-iron gazebos in the field outside Belmont Community Centre. It would be wrong to be too dismissive of this type of construction, because a lot of future council voters should be very grateful for them. These things were almost never used for the purpose for which they were intended but they were very good places to go if you wanted to be undisturbed, and a lot of new life saw its first few seconds here as teenage sperm met teenage egg.

Right up at the other end of the scale was the cash-guzzling white mammoth that came to be known as the Gala Theatre. The Gala Theatre deserves a whole book to itself, but it is almost certain never to be written because the documentation "sleeps with the hamsters" as I outlined in the Introduction. The whole concept of this entertainment complex was surrounded by controversy long before the first brick was ever laid, when the Cobbler's Window first displayed the scandal of The Sacred Journey film contract. Precisely why this one million pound contract was given to affluent Shincliffe resident Brendan Quayle without it going out to public tender remains a mystery to this day.

The story published in Private Eye would have us believe that a group of people came together to play tennis on a regular basis, and as a result of this the old pals act kicked in and somehow the contract was awarded. The group consisted of Gerry

Steinberg, Brendan Quayle, Colin Shearsmith, and a few of the other Usual Suspects, possibly including a senior policeman called Suddes. My disbelief of this theory is based upon having watched some of these people attempt to play tennis. Most of them can hardly hit a ball, and therefore I regard the theory that they have played regularly at some time in the past as somewhat implausible.

Somehow or other Brendan Quayle was awarded the contract to make a film called "The Sacred Journey" in large-screen I-Max format as a centrepiece of the Gala Theatres cinema section, despite protests from a number of knowledgeable people, because the Council wilfully flouted EC rules. I quote from one of these " I believe that the value of the contract exceeds the threshold of £584,901, (set out in directive 97/52/EC) which requires a mandatory PIN to be issued by the Council. In any event no advertisement of any kind or any sort of transparent procurement process has been undertaken. No one other than Dr Quayle has been invited to bid for this prestigious work."

It goes on to say "The CEO of Durham City Council, Mr Colin Shearsmith is Director of the Joint-Venture Company: the City Council, in partnership with AMEC Development. (The City Council has signed a 250-year lease of the Walkergate site to AMEC Development in return for £12.5 million matching funding for the Millennium City Development. The Millennium Commission grant of £12.5 million, was dependent on matching funding). **The City Council is therefore doubly culpable in its evasion of EC environmental procurement requirements."**

Councillors were told that Mr Quayle had been given the contract without it going to tender because he was the only person in the world who was capable of doing it, which is simply not true - mushroom management! The Councillors were either kept in ignorance, or simply ignored the remarkable coincidence that this unique individual just happened to be a friend of Shearmith and Steinberg. The fact is that money was given to Quayle by Durham City Council, well in advance of the announcement that a film was to be made, and they even financed his fact-finding mission to the USA so that he was in a position to buy equipment to enable him to put in a pre-production contract for the film. As it happens the full contract never went out to tender anyway, thus bypassing any awkward questions.

Around about this time awkward questions started to be asked. I quote "Indeed, the precise chronology of decisions by the City Council requires clarification...... Subsequently I understand that Mr Quayle has been appointed as film producer for the main contract worth hundreds of Thousands of pounds. It appears that he has effectively been subsidised by the taxpayer to research the IMAX market and put himself in a position to be awarded the main contract. Why was this main contract not put out to competitive tender? ......Underpinning the above points is one fact: it is well known in Durham that Mr Quayle is a personal friend of Mr Shearsmith"

Another Hutton-style whitewash by the District Auditor, Mr Parkin, conveniently appears to omit the fact that Quayle had been given finance by the Council to purchase equipment a year in advance of Quayle being gift-wrapped the contract. When the embarrassing friendship between Quayle and Shearsmith was made public by "Mac" McWilliams (see "A Black Cloud Looms") in the BBC Close-Up North documentary, Shearsmith denied any friendship, stating publicly that he had only met Quayle on a couple of occasions playing tennis. "Mac" McWilliams stated on TV that Shearsmith had asked him to arrange to have the boiler fixed in Quayle's luxurious Shincliffe home. Dr Quayle most certainly does not live in a council house - why use council workers for somebody Shearsmith allegedly did not know? Why did the auditor fail to report these facts, which may have rendered the whole thing criminal?

All right, we are looking at this with the benefit of hindsight, but a lot of big mistakes have been made by people who were paid a great deal of money to advise the Council. Preliminary feasibility studies suggested that around 100,000 people per year would visit the Gala to see this film, and spend money in the bar and restaurant as well. The estimated revenue was around £400,000 per year of which Dr Quayle would receive about £50,000 for his twelve-and-a quarter percent of his copyright of Durham's historical heritage. Go figure, Doc!

So much for feasibility studies, because figures in February 2004's Private Eye reveals that last year's income from The Sacred Journey amounted to just £7,314, or about 2 people in each of the 700 screenings and on a memorable occasion I was one of those people.

For whatever reason, £1 million pounds was spent on The Sacred Journey film, with Quayle's family appearing in the cast. There are those who believe that one million pounds was a lot of money to spend on a film like this, but I disagree. I have seen The Sacred Journey and I think it was money well spent. It must have cost a fraction of the budget of the only other film that caused me to laugh out loud in recent times, which was "The Mask" starring Jim Carrey. The acting and the characters are reminiscent of the Monty Python sketch about the Crusades, "The Knights Who Say Ni." My laughter was obviously disturbing the only other person in the audience, a young lady who seemed to be attempting to have a deep spiritual experience, which was what the film advertised itself to be. Not wishing to disturb her, and knowing that it was unlikely that I could stop myself laughing, I left.

I am aware of the fact that it demeans great art to talk about it in terms of money, but now that we are eighteen months down the line from its premiere we can start looking at the financial consequences of Brendan Quayle's creation. In its first year of screening it took £7,000 in gate receipts but the projectionist was paid £27,000 for showing it. Interesting statistic number one is therefore that the people of Durham City would be £20,000 per year or £400 per week better off if this film was never shown again, all aesthetic considerations apart.

If this continues then Dr Quayle's epic production will lose money to the tune of about £140 every time it is shown for the next ten years.

As a postscript to this story, in Autumn 2003 I felt the need to get away from people and that the best thing to do would be to go and see Sacred Journey film again. For some reason I was more impressed by it this time, and feel that I must put the record straight by saying so. When looked at objectively it is not as bad as I thought the first time I saw it, but certainly not (in my humble opinion at least) worth one million pounds of taxpayers' money when you consider what could have been done with that money otherwise. Possibly at the very heart of a lot of criticism of that film is the fact that a lot of Durham citizens believe that the story which is at the very heart of the creation of our city, the spiritual roots of Durham City if you like, have been taken and prostituted for someone's financial gain. Anyway, enough of all that, let us go on to look at other aspects of the story of our theatre.

The opening night of the Gala Theatre set the tone for what was to come. If you want know how to spend about £70,000 in one night and have nothing to show for it, other than a bar-room floor that sticks to the soles of your feet as you walk over it, then ask Colin Shearsmith. Precise details of the financial catastrophe that occurred that night are unavailable at this point in time, and it may be significant that the Entertainment Team (Durham) Limited (ETDL)claim that Shearsmith was reluctant to have detailed minutes of meetings taken, and why Nick Rule decided to go into meetings with Shearsmith with a minidisk recorder in his pocket. Of course, there is also the question of the bin bags full of hamster bedding that may or may not have departed from the Council offices early in the morning after the LibDem election victory.

From the very outset the Council were anxious to give the impression that the theatre was being run at arm's length from the Council itself so a management team,

Entertainment Team (Durham) Limited, was hired. The directors of this team were Nick Rule and Mike Power. Despite their names, Rule and Power- what tremendous names for managers - these men were inexperienced and had very little capital behind them. The company they set up had a very thin financial shell because it was not intended to incur losses, its job was simply to manage the theatre and pass any bills on to Colin Shearsmith who, at this stage, had given an undertaking that the City Council would underwrite any financial losses. The contract did not include any clauses about financial penalties for Rule and Power, simply stating that they could be sacked if things went wrong and things were most certainly going wrong, at about 9.9 on the Richter cock-up scale of ten. "I can categorically state that neither the board of the company nor its directors would have contemplated entering into a management contract of the sort proposed without assurances of funding by the owners of the venue" Nick Rule states.

The fact is that the greed of the Councillors themselves destroyed the concept of an independent management company, which essentially went bust on the night the theatre opened. Shearsmith wanted a spectacular opening to put the theatre on the map, and a budget of £70,000 was allocated. The band Westlife was hired to give a concert, which was a popular move. So popular, in fact that 60% of the seats were immediately snapped up as freebies for Councillors and their guests. On average each non-paying councillor brought four non-paying guests, which meant that it became impossible for the opening night to run at a profit.

In an attempt to offset this, a giant screen simultaneous broadcast of the event at nearby Gilesgate Sixth Form Centre was planned but was dogged with problems from the start, not the least of which was that the young people of Durham wanted to see Westlife in person. After all that is what theatre is all about, watching real live famous people stand up on stage and perform for you. Most of them were unable to get tickets for the live event because the councillors had got there first and frustrated by this they stayed away from the simultaneous telecast in droves.

Colin Shearsmith started to panic because he was beginning to realise that things were going wrong and started blaming Rule and Power. The publicity was bad, the artwork poor - these were the reasons things were looking bad, and in Shearsmith's opinion it was entirely the fault of ETDL. The fact was that if he was unable to shift the blame it would fall upon himself and Crathorne, and the best-case scenario was that the pair of them would look complete fools. The worst-case scenario was that Crathorne could be surcharged for allowing the public to incur an excessive financial debt and Shearsmith was not about to let that happen.

The opening night was upon them. The biggest mistake of all seems to have been giving free drinks to the councillors, because unconsumed free alcohol to a Durham councillor is like a red rag to a bull. It is an insult to their northern masculinity, something that must be got rid of as soon as possible. At the beginning of the night some attempt was made to keep a track of who was drinking what, but in the middle of the frenzy around the bar, the staff could do nothing other than hand out drinks as the enormous pile of free-drinks chitties kept falling over onto the alcopop soaked floor.

Staff who dared to protest that some councillors had had more than their allowance were bullied into silence. For some staff this was their first and last night of employment. The luckier ones lasted until the bar became the first victim of the Gala Theatre mismanagement, going bankrupt three months later in spite of strategies such as sending junior staff out to the local Bottoms Up off-licence to buy cheap own-brand spirits to put in the Grouse and Teachers optics. When the cost was finally counted it became plain that on the opening night councillors had apparently treated themselves to freebies worth about £650 per head. A brave decision from people who had voted to cancel disabled parking in the centre of Durham City and Meals-on-Wheels to save money, then voted themselves free parking in the city's car parks. The headline of the Evening Chronicle echoed the words of the people of Durham City - "Hypocrites!"

The Chronicle did not know the true extent of the hypocrisy, though. It takes a lot to shock your average Durham Councillor, but when foxy Maurice Crathorne proposed a motion during a City Council meeting that they should stop the Meals-on-Wheels service to pay for a 20% pay rise for the City Council officers, there was a pin-drop silence throughout the chamber. By all accounts the only opposition came from down-to-earth ex-Mayor, Joe Anderson, who was subsequently deselected, after many years' service to the City, for attempting to stand up and tell the truth along with his longtime colleague Ian Fawcett. These two have remained the backbone of the political opposition to the Gala scandal ever since. Meals-on-Wheels stopped and the officers received their 20% pay rise.

By now it was apparent to them that the losses incurred during the Gala's opening night had crippled Rule and Power's ETDL financially and the resulting cash-flow problems meant that their lives were simply one long series of arguments with creditors. The strain was beginning to tell on the pair and Mike Power was already ill. Nick Rule took over the bulk of the administration but the stress was starting to take its toll upon him as well, and this previously robust man started to slip into the bouts of anxiety and depression, which can be the only explanation for some of his subsequent actions.

Shearsmith was apoplectic with panic by now because the Gala Theatre was open but not all of its services were working yet, a major breach in the contract conditions of ETDL. Theatrical productions were being staged but the kitchens were not open so visitors could not eat, and Brendan Quayle's Sacred Journey film was not completed. Staff had been hired, but were standing around with nothing to do, but still needed to be paid and ETDL was slipping further into the red. Shearsmith seemed to be blaming Liz Hall, the City's Finance Director for part of the problem and started denigrating her as a council officer in the presence of Rule and Power and in all probability he was bad-mouthing Rule and Power when talking to Ms Hall.

The ETDL team spoke to Natwest Bank manger Rob Salt who was demanding repayment of money borrowed from them and asked when the Durham City Council money would be arriving, as the Theatre was now well over their overdraft limit. Rule and Power spoke to Liz Hall's City Treasurer's Office, who assured them that the money was on its way. A few minutes later a fax arrived at the London office of Rule and Power from Liz Hall's office containing a company guarantee to pay the full £50,000 with two personal guarantees attached. Nick Rule spoke to Liz Hall's assistant who explained that no money would be released until the guarantees were signed and faxed back. They tried to speak to senior staff at Durham City Council but nobody was available, and they finally got to speak to Mrs Jackson of the Finance Department who said that City Council Solicitor Lesley Blackie had told her that such an arrangement was routine and simply a formality.

Rob Salt from Natwest was getting more anxious and made several phone calls to Rule and Power demanding the payment. They were forced to sign the guarantees and fax them back. Straight after the faxes the money was paid but Rule and Power were adamant that they would not sign the hard copy of these guarantees. Shearsmith's next response was to call a series of acrimonious meetings with Nick Rule, attempting to force him to take on a series of further personal financial guarantees which he alleged would help bail out ETDL and save Rule's job. Nick Rule was having none of it, and became suspicious of the fact that Shearsmith was refusing to allow any written records of the meetings until the financial situation improved. Meanwhile City Council Leader Maurice Crathorne, aware of the fact that criticisms of Shearsmith's excessive secretiveness was already on its way to the Local Government Ombudsman, let him get on with it, conniving in Shearsmith's cover-up of the real financial situation to the City Council.

Rule and Power still believe that "the nature of the fraud was that Officers (Shearsmith and Co) already knew when negotiating with directors (Rule and Power) that members (Councillors) were not prepared to financially support the level of risk...........and put us at risk that we would be trading the company from day one in an insolvent position......We had no other sources of financial support.......I am sure that members had been misled all along about the financial risks to the City and its taxpayers. As it is the venue was operated by a £100 company with no assets......the actual evidence points directly at the City as being culpable. **We were merely too trusting of the integrity of public servants"**

By early 2002 Nick Rule was close to the brink of despair, and that is the only possible explanation for what happened next. It was the day of the official opening of the theatre, and the streets of Durham had been swept to sparkling perfection ready for the arrival of HRH Queen Elizabeth. In a bizarre incident that occurred literally two minutes before the official opening in the Gala Theatre on 7th May, City Solicitor Lesley Blackie and City Treasurer Liz Hall cornered Nick Rule and virtually twisted his arm up his back to sign a series of documents which meant that Rule himself took on a crippling series of personal financial guarantees. In what can only be classified as some sort of momentary lapse of reason on his part Nick Rule signed them, and thereby sealed his own fate.

I have met the two ladies in question and I can visualise what might have gone on that day. You can almost see the two of them in their black wide-shouldered power dressing outfits, cornering him and poking him with bony fingers, Macbeth-witch style.

"You are being very stubborn, Nicholas. Make it easy for yourself and sign the documents."

"Yes, Nicholas, sign. Go on, sign - we have ways of making you sign, you know!"

"Yes, Nicholas, this wilfulness must stop now. Sign these documents or we will not let the Queen in!"

In desperation Nick Rule signs just to get rid of them and the two speed away cackling as they go to show Shearsmith what they have done, pausing only to mix themselves a freebie gin and tonic from behind the bar complete with Eye of Newt on a cocktail stick. In fact that particular sketch is in very bad taste because the documents Nick Rule signed that day transferred the financial blame away from Shearsmith and Crathorne and onto himself, and it was only later that he began to realise the enormity of his foolishness. When Nick Rule tackled Shearsmith about sending the two Council harpies to extract the hard guarantees from him, Shearsmith was characteristically unsympathetic. **"You are in it now"** he sneered, relieved that he had managed to shift the blame onto the two unsuspecting managers. Later he told a Council meeting that "The directors had *offered* personal guarantees to support them"

What seems most suspicious of all is Shearsmith's denial that written minutes of all of these meetings were taken. Rule and Power allege that extensive minutes were taken by City Council officers at every meeting, but they seem to have disappeared. Where have they all gone - is it possible that they now "sleep with the hamsters?"

Unfortunately for Shearsmith Nick Rule had a trick up his sleeve. He had lost confidence in the oily Chief Executive Officer, and had decided to carry a tiny minidisk recorder in his pocket whenever they met and there are hours of incriminating conversations. It is not difficult to understand the Council's concern when they found out about Nick Rule's recordings as this example might demonstrate. In this short excerpt from a transcript of one of them - **NR** is Nick Rule, **CS** is Colin Shearsmith and **LH** is Liz Hall, Finance Director of Durham City Council. Nick Rule has compiled a letter asking Colin Shearsmith for £50,000 for a breach in the contract.

> **NR** "I'd like to show you a letter which has been drafted at the request of the board and which I haven't sent."

> **CS** "To?"

> **NR** "To Lesley (*Blackie, Legal Director*). Under the terms of our contract there is a right to recover costs for failure of the City to deliver a complete venue. The Board genuinely think that the time has come to recover the real costs to the business for not having the venue complete. There are £50k in costs just to the beginning of February….."

> **CS** "How is this made up?"

> **NR** "Have a look at the breakdown"

> *(Silence as Shearsmith reads the document)*

CS "Well, This would not be well received."

NR "I wanted to show you it before sending it."

CS "As far as I'm concerned there have been some difficulties which we are trying to resolve.... we've been bending over backwards**.... If you hold us to the letter of the contract I will send my legal people. I believe you will not live long enough to enforce it.**"

NR "Err...."

CS *(Very angry)* "I would be very disappointed if they got that letter."

NR "That's why I have shown it to you before anyone else."

CS "Well it will not give progression to our situation, not by any means."

LH "If you had been able to prove it to me, and we had known about it, we could have come up with cash. If you had said, hand on heart what the problem was and justified it.... the problem is that...

NR "Come off it, Liz."

I would have loved to have been a fly on the wall of Colin Shearsmith's living room when this was broadcast by the BBC in their Inside Out documentary on 9th February 2004! What this documentary did prove is that the Council were fully aware of the finances of the Theatre, a fact that they strenuously denied in the press after the financial collapse of ETDL.

Although Nick Rule has massive amounts of evidence to show that he was tricked by the officers of Durham City Council he is having difficulty taking them to court because it is expensive to do so and he has been made bankrupt. He has joined one of a growing number of people whose lives and health have been destroyed by the corrupt actions of City and County Council officers and members. Meanwhile back at the Gala Theatre, after ETDL went tits-up, the management went directly into the hands of Colin Shearsmith and Maurice Crathorne, and through their wise administration it started to turn over a massive profit and they all rode off into the sunset and lived happily ever after. **In your dreams, Maurice.**

By May 2002 the Cobbler's shop was buzzing with all sorts of wild allegations about the Gala goings-on. Source after reliable source was telling him that the Gala was about to go tits-up and eventually he came to believe it and contacted the BBC. The BBC contacted Christine Holland who denied anything was wrong, and the denials continued until later that evening when a press release finally admitted that ETDL had been forced into debts of more than £700,000. Tony the Cobbler could smell a rat, and as the dust started to settle he received more not-for-publication documents that showed how the Council intended to "cherry-pick" its most important Gala Theatre creditors for payment. For instance Durham Amateur Operatic Society were repaid £9,000 but the African Children's Choir look likely to receive none of the £1,400 they are owed. The injustice of this urged the Cobbler to confront the Economic Crime Unit (aka Fraud Squad) of Durham Constabulary.

Eventually a meeting with Sergeant Hall took place, and Tony made his suspicions known. Paperwork was passed over and the Cobbler demanded an investigation. The Gala Theatre liquidator, Mr Marlor, eventually contacted the Cobbler and passed details on to Rule and Power, who contacted the Cobbler, the first of a long series of dialogues. Time passed with no progress and the Cobbler contacted the Fraud Squad again, this time Mr Gibson. Head of the Fraud Squad, responded. "If the Liquidator finds something wrong we will investigate" he reported. The faint smell of bullshit wafted towards the Cobbler's nostrils, a smell he was becoming increasingly familiar with. He contacted Marlor the Liquidator who denied that the Police had made any such arrangement. Requests were made for this to be put in writing, but nothing was done for the next seven months, when the Cobbler wrote to the Chief Constable, naming those who held the evidence relating to the Gala fraud.

On May 3rd a letter came back from Gibson saying that "They were not into fishing expeditions and there was no evidence to substantiate an investigation," Tony now knew this was bullshit because by now he had the evidence, and now there has been a complaint logged against Mr Gibson of the Fraud Squad for failing to investigate these crimes. Tony has since tried to lodge a complaint against the Chief Constable and Assistant Chief Constable Ron Hogg with Durham Police Authority, but the Police Authority refused to log it, even though County Council Officers Andrew North and Kingsley Smith have both stated that the Chief Constable is acting illegally by not recording one of Tony's main complaints. Has the Police Authority ever accepted a complaint against its Chief Constable? What is the use of the expensive complaints process if it is never used?

Tony contacted the Chief Constable on 20th August 2003 to log a complaint for failing to investigate the Gala collapse, and allegations of fraud by a prominent Labour Councillor. Yet another Constabulary member, Inspector Redshaw was called in to "investigate" the Cobbler's allegations. For the benefit of those who do not know him, Inspector Redshaw is a big man, six foot seven inches of rippling muscle and long curly dark eyelashes, plus size fourteen feet. "You know what they say about men with big feet?" the Cobbler enquired at their first meeting.

"What's that?" snapped Redshaw, anxious to get down to business.

"Big feet, big Cobbler's bills" replied the Cobbler. A big grin spread across the face of the gigantic Hagrid look-alike officer. The day was 23rd October, and the Cobbler had a lot to smile about, because he knew that down in London Rule and Power were presenting their damning evidence to the Metropolitan Police, accompanied by a member of the Durham business community.

"Come on then Tony, what sort of **tangible** evidence have you got?" Redshaw asked. Tangible was his favourite word.

"I've got this transcript of a tape recording. It's being presented to the Met as we speak, Mr Redshaw." the Cobbler replied. Mr Redshaw paled visibly, and appeared to shrink to about five foot tall. "Is that **tangible** enough, Mr Redsaw?" the Cobbler teased.

"Well, I'll have to get back to Headquarters and check out whether what you have told me is correct" the large Inspector replied. A cheery goodbye, and stooping down to avoid banging his head on the top of the door, he was gone. Tony knew it was true, but he was also aware that things were not as might have been hoped in the new LibDem City Council cabinet. Bit by bit news was leaking out about a Halloween staff party at the Gala, which had come to an abrupt end with one member of staff having to be taken to hospital after collapsing. Later it transpired that cannabis-laced cake had been passed around and she had suffered an overdose. An ambulance was called and she was taken away. Shearsmith was in the shit because he had sanctioned the party and Jan Mathin, the acting manager, had told staff that if news of this sorry incident leaked out, they would be sacked. Later she herself was sacked for gross misconduct relating to this incident. The LibDem Cabinet were not happy and an emergency meeting was called.

LibDem Leader Sue Pitts, fresh from a trip to Sri Lanka, was rapidly brought up to speed on the situation and Shearsmith was summoned. The exact details of the meeting are uncertain, but by the end it is alleged that Shearsmith was given the ultimatum of leaving the Council's employment on the grounds of ill health or being suspended and an internal enquiry held. "Can I have time to think about it?" Shearsmith is reported to have asked.

"No," came the reply "we want your answer now."

"I'll take the ill-health" was Shearsmith's alleged reply. It was decided that Shearsmith would leave in the near future, and the Cobbler had found out about the whole story, and wasn't having any of it.

"How can we stop this bastard slipping out of the back door?" thought the Cobbler. Fortunately, circumstances had occurred that would prevent this. Rule and Power's tape recording transcript of the infamous meeting where Shearsmith threatens Nick Rule, and the Met-briefing document containing the formal allegations against Shearsmith, Lesley Blackie and Liz Hall had been handed over to County Councillor Barbara Howarth, who is also a City Councillor. For some reason this evidence was given to City Council solicitor Lesley Blackie, who was actually the subject of the allegations, who in turn passed it on to Colin Shearsmith, also named in the allegations.

Subsequently it was discovered that they had obtained this vital information from none other than LibDem Leader Sue Pitts, who had been given it by Barbara Howarth. This was reported to Durham Police as a possible conspiracy to pervert the course of justice by three different Durham City residents, but as usual the police have refused to investigate.

The following Monday all hell broke loose. Shearsmith was apparently given this damning evidence by Lesley Blackie and took off like a scalded cat. He was due to attend a Gala Theatre scrutiny meeting that evening, but presented his apologies due to illness and high blood pressure. Perhaps he had just seen Nick Rule's transcript of the meeting where he had threatened him - high blood pressure material for anybody! By this time Tony Jones of Radio Newcastle had scented something and was hot on the trail, but Mr Jones and the rest of the public were excluded from all but the first few minutes of the meeting. So much for LibDem openness, transparency and honesty. Sue Pitts stated on the BBC documentary of 9th February that "her officers had done nothing wrong" and denied all of the ETDL allegations. This woman is a liar and it will be proved in the civil courts. Notice that we are not saying **criminal** courts - not with coppers like the ones we have now.

18th December 2003 saw yet another meeting at the Town Hall, this time a full

Council Meeting. Each Councillor was given a piece of paper with details of Shearsmith's retirement package on it. Each piece of paper had the Councillor's name on it, and they were counted back in to make sure that there was no possibility of this information leaking to the public. By all accounts Sue Pitts and Carol Woods tried to convince the meeting that this massive payout was in the best interests of the taxpayer, while simultaneously preventing the taxpayer getting to know about it. Not surprising, because the alleged costs of Shearsmith's hurried departure were £278,000 plus Shearsmith's £1,000 per week pension.

February 2004 and the Gala Theatre remains a massive problem for the people of Durham City. The Council has been forced to reveal that the operating loss for the theatre over the past year amounts to three-quarters of a million pounds, and will probably remain at this level as long as it is open. The Council has appointed a management team from Darlington to take over the running at more expense to the taxpayer. What is apparent is that there has been a mass fraud perpetrated upon the people of Durham City, the whole of the upper structure must be aware of this and sooner or later this will come to light. In the meantime the cover-up continues with Deputy CEO Brian Spears moving up to fill Shearsmith's shoes, and he cannot have been unaware of what Shearsmith was up to. His former post has been made redundant to pay for Shearsmith's massive pension benefits.

LibDem City Council Leader Sue Pitts, who was part of the original Labour-controlled cabinet decision making team responsible for sanctioning the ill-fated Millennium City Development, continues to cover up the truth.

Overall what comes through very strongly is that the key decisions in relation to the setting up and operation of the Gala Theatre appear to have been made by only a handful of people, probably less than five, including CEO Colin Shearsmith, and then rubber-stamped by the rest of the councillors. What is even more worrying is that the councillors themselves believed that it was appropriate that no written records should be kept of the meetings between Shearsmith and the Entertainment Team (Durham) Limited management team, even after he had been criticised as "secretive" by the local government ombudsman.

A situation like this would have been much less likely to have happened prior to Blair's reformation of the structure of local government into the current leader-and-cabinet version we have now, with most of the elected councillors relegated to the role of toothless scrutinisers of decisions already made behind closed doors. Over and over again you are forced to the conclusion that the five most corrupt councillors are chosen, numbers one and two become Cabinet Leader and Deputy while the other three are sent off to chair (read "pull the wool over the eyes of") the scrutiny committees.

Of course, faced with the alternative of owning up to being part of a criminal conspiracy to defraud the people of Durham City or being thought so stupid that you were unaware that anything untoward was going on, the queue headed "Stoopid Councillors stand here" stretches three times around the block. Right at the head of this queue and already dressed for the part in his bulbous red nose and floppy clown shoes has got to be Steven Laverick, ex-Deputy Leader of the Council. All I can say is that if your house is on fire and the man running towards you, hosepipe in hand, is Fireman Steve, my advice to you has got to be to find your home insurance policy and keep it safe because it looks like you're going to need it. Do the good people of Durham a favour, Fire Brigade, and put Fireman Steve on permanent duty manning those fire engines you send to church fetes for the kids to climb over. That is about all he seems to be capable of handling.

Who is that standing behind him, is it Crusty the Clown? No, it is none other than Joe Knight, chairman of the biggest of the scrutiny committees, whose job it was to make sure that Crathorne, Laverick and the rest of the council cabinet were doing their job properly. Listen carefully and you can hear him rehearsing his excuses under his breath, deciding just where to place the emphasis on his words to make them a bit more believable. "Don't blame *me*. I didn't do it. Don't blame me. *I* didn't do it. Don't blame me. I *didn't* do it. *Don't* blame me. I didn't do it." What have you got to say to all of the people of Durham City who are saying that keeping an eye on the cabinet to prevent corrupt dealings was your job, Joe?

"Don't blame me, **I didn't do it**," says Joe. I thought so. Well there you are, that's what happens when you put a fifteen million pound building project in the hands of a bunch of clowns.

Who is that right at the end of the queue, pretending that she shouldn't be there at all? Why it's Sue Pitts, the LibDem lady we all voted in to do something about this scandal. She's there because though she is aware of the full enormity of the scandal she has done absolutely nothing about it. Many of us are suspicious of the fact that Maurice Crathorne made this lady part of his cabinet in that final year before Labour was swept from power, which was an uncharacteristic show of generosity.

The suspicion remains that he did so only in return for the promise of some sort of amnesty if and when the unthinkable happened and the Labour-run City Council was swept from power. Faced with the likelihood of the full extent of political

66

corruption in Durham coming to light, did Maurice Crathorne show Sue Pitts where the tastiest morsels in the Durham City trough were to be found, and in return did she promise not to look into past misdemeanours too deeply?

Of course no good mystery story would be complete without a devious lawyer, and ours is no exception. There, skulking in the shadows is Lesley Blackie, the City Council's legal eagle. Wait a minute, its not an eagle at all, it's a vulture! No, hang on a minute, it is very difficult to see her in this light, she may even be a turkey. In any event Ms Blackie is the one who is guarding the true secrets of the Millennium City from all prying eyes, including those of the new LibDem Councillors apparently. Come on, LibDems, if you are at all serious about finding out the truth about the Gala Theatre debacle, the first step has got to be to give Lesley Blackie a black plastic bin-bag and tell her to take nothing else from her desk other than er potted plant and other personal knick-knacks, then make her eligible for Unemployment Benefit. It's about time, and the good people of Durham City need to know just what has happened to all of their Council Tax. Do it now before a civil action forces Durham to repay £25 million to the Millennium Commission, which seems almost inevitable at this point.

Why don't you just close the Gala Theatre down and have done with it? Well, remember that this cannot be done because it would mean paying something like £15 million back to the Lottery Commission, which the City Council cannot afford to do because it would bankrupt it. The Gala Theatre reminds me of the creature in the Alien series of films that has acid for blood that is capable of eating through the hull of your spacecraft if you try to kill it. If they do nothing the running costs of the Theatre will eventually eat them up, but they simply cannot afford to kill this insatiable white cash-guzzler so the council has decided to bide their time and feed it vast amounts of taxpayers' money while hoping they will not notice it. In its first year of operations it swallowed about £900,000 and it is difficult to see just how that figure could be reduced significantly.

I am aware that the Gala Theatre is a tremendous cultural asset to Durham City and that I am likely to be branded as a philistine for being so critical of it. The fact is that I have attended a number of performances at The Gala Theatre and have enjoyed every one immensely, so much in fact that it has re-awakened my interest in live theatre. Unfortunately my enjoyment is always tempered when I realise that the majority of people in Durham are unable to afford the typical entry price of about £14 per ticket, and therefore my entertainment is being heavily subsidised by people poorer than myself through the mechanism of the council tax. Yes I enjoy the drama and the spectacle but I am aware of the people

on low fixed incomes who are driven to distraction by the spiralling tax demands
caused in part by my pleasure, and this brings the unreformed socialist inside me
back up to the surface.

Yes, we need culture but above all we must be sensitive to the needs of others, especially those who are not as fortunate as ourselves. I love the dramatic white façade of the Gala Theatre, but I am also conscious of my belief that the main reason it was brought into being was so that the councillors, officers and assorted hangers-on could benefit from the process and it is likely to be a financial millstone around the neck of generations of citizens of Durham who will never ever see the inside of it. You pays your money and you takes your choice? Well the first bit is right anyway.

Meanwhile, back in the Land of the Prince Bishops the Cobbler has displayed in his window a letter from 10 Downing Street sent to a prominent Labour Party member who has asked Tony Blair to investigate corruption in Durham.. The letter says that unfortunately Mr Blair is too busy (or too shrewd?) to get involved in another MP's affairs, so he has passed it on to Gerry Steinberg MP and Labour North for them to investigate. Thank you for your ongoing concern and hard work on behalf of the Labour Party, signed Caroline Adams, dated 17th August 2001. Has ex-City Councillor Gerry Steinberg MP investigated these allegations? Not as of this date, which is Sunday 19th October 2003.

Ah well, that's entertainment.

Finally, remember that not all council megalomania ends up being expressed bricks and mortar style. When our Councillors heard that Ken Livingstone was about to introduce a congestion charge in London, a childhood ambition to be in The Guinness Book of Records must have resurfaced somewhere. You can almost hear the shrill clamours of "Let's get in there before Ken, let's be first!" echoing through the ancient beamed roof at the Town Hall. That is how we got the congestion charge on cars going up to the cathedral peninsula, along with the infamous Cathedral Bus Service. In fact they were in such a hurry to beat Ken Livingstone that the tollgate was installed two months before the formal decision by the Secretary of State was made.

This is how Durham got its dreaded car-eating toll barrier in the Market Place, which seems to be destroying an average of a car per week by popping up at unpredictable times, and has even speared a police car through its unsuspecting bonnet. There have been so many incidents that Fred Henderson, who runs the largest of the local breakdown recovery services in the area was quoted on the front page of the Durham Advertiser saying that a safer barrier was needed. Durham County Council spokesperson Mr Wafer blamed the carelessness of the drivers, and that the Bollard from Hell as it has now come to be known was totally blameless.

Initially it was estimated that the County Council would make £5000 per day from the toll charges, but on the first full day of operation 200 out of the 300 who passed the barrier were able to claim exemption from the charge, the overall result being that only £200 was taken. Now that the Council has been forced to have human supervision of this so-called automatic barrier this is going to eat into the takings even more, and the only one who can pick up the bill is the taxpayer.

Then there is the Cathedral Bus service of course. You need to be a special sort of person to drive a Cathedral Bus in Durham, and probably only redundant lighthouse keepers can stand the loneliness of the job. My heart goes out to these solitary individuals, because it must be absolutely soul-destroying to drive a completely empty bus around Durham all day. The Labour Party tried to make the situation look better in the run-up to the City Council election by encouraging Party members to ride in the Cathedral Bus as well as go to Gala Theatre, but the scheme convinced nobody. A letter in the Durham Advertiser summed it up. "I have seen a passenger on a Cathedral Bus. Is that a record?"

I have done my best to make the facts in this book as accurate as possible, and therefore I feel that it is necessary to put the record straight. Passengers on the Cathedral Bus are by no means as rare as this letter would have us believe. In a previously unpublished survey (carried out by myself) I can tell you that, on average, about one bus in sixteen carries a passenger. The survey method was to sit in the Market Place and watch the Cathedral Bus go past. Thirty-two buses went past until one was seen with an elderly couple enjoying their journey.

Have you got nothing else to do apart from watching empty Cathedral Buses go past, you may be asking? All I can say is that they have closed the cinema down, turned it into an Australian theme pub and the only alternative viewing is The Sacred Journey. Which would you choose?

Chapter 6
The Wrong Arm of the Law

It's been an unusually busy day for me. Early this morning (well, 10am is early for me) my mobile phone rang. Picking it up, I noticed the message on the screen, "Cobbler Mobile." "Hi, Tony" I said, trying to sound glad at being disturbed by him at this hour on a nice Sunday morning.

"Look, there's a guy up at Ushaw Moor who says that there is some dodgy stuff going on. Get up there and sort him out, will you?" I have put the question mark there for the sake of grammar, but in reality it sounded less like a request than an order. "It's a guy called Haggett, High View, Ushaw Moor." Before I have time to tell him that it is Sunday morning and I am still slightly hung over, my phone tells me that the call is over and it took fourteen seconds. OK, on with the motley.

Soon I am speeding up to pleasant rural Ushaw Moor on the outskirts of Durham City as fast as my aging car will allow. Within ten minutes I arrive on the steps of 28 High View, Ushaw Moor. Knocking on the door I am greeted by a pleasant smiling gentleman in his middle years and I begin the well-rehearsed speech.

"Good morning, my name is John Doe and I am an investigative researcher working on behalf of Tony Martin, the Durham Cobbler. Mr Martin tells me that you have a Council Cock-Up to report."

"Yes, that's right" the gentleman beams. "Please come in."

"Ah, just wait a moment, please" I respond. "First we have got to make sure that we have a genuine Council Cock-Up." I ruffle through the documents in my tattered Tesco carrier bag until I reach the check-list entitled *Typical Council Cock-Up.*

"Now then, just a few questions. Question Number One, has your problem been going on for years and years, and is it no closer to being solved now than it was at the beginning?" A nod and a tick in the box. Good - you've got to keep on top of the paperwork in this job because it soon mounts up, you know.

"Question Two, have you got hundreds and hundreds of bits of paper in bags, boxes and folders, lying all over the house?" Another nod, another tick.

"Question Three, Does it seem from your experience that the left hand of the council neither knows nor cares what the right hand is doing?" Nod, tick.

"Question Four, have you got lots of letters from condescending overpaid council solicitors who seem to assume that you are some sort of fool because you do not have a Law Degree, and therefore cannot see that they are trying to take you for a ride? " I take some papers from his hand, look at them briefly, then tick boxes labelled Andrew North, Lesley Blackie.

"Question Five, did things really start to go badly tits-up when Mr John Prescott, or one of the many Ministries run by Mr Prescott, got involved?" Look at papers, tick box labelled DEFRA.

"Thank you, now finally Question Number Six.. Have you tried just about everything else and in desperation been reduced to taking your problem to one of those toothless ombudsmen people who takes ages and ages, then finally comes up with some sort of recommendation that is nothing more than just a recommendation, and the Council is free to ignore in any case?"

The gentleman's eyes light up in the realisation that he is not alone in his problems. "Yes, that's right. How did you know?"

"Thank you, Mr Haggett, you have scored six out of six and it looks as if we do indeed have a genuine Council Cock-Up here. Now if you can just sign here, underneath the bit that says *It is my true and honest belief that I am simply being fobbed off by a load of time-wasting council paper-pushers in the hope that I will eventually get fed up and go away, or perhaps simply die of old age. Please reveal this scandal to the public on my behalf.* Yes, that's right, just there. Thank you very much. Congratulations, you are now entitled to a free one-page entry in the Cobbler's new book, Cobblers to the Council."

I am escorted into a pleasant well-furnished living room, and as always spend a moment wondering if indeed I am the only person in the world whose home is in perpetual and total chaos. Dragged back to reality I notice that there are the obligatory bits of documentary evidence lying on the spotless floor, waiting for my inspection. Bit by bit the story is revealed and I scrawl it onto sheet after sheet of paper in my large spidery-like longhand. It seems like a fairly typical combined City and County Council cock-up, with all the Usual Suspects involved.

Over the next fifteen minutes the eight yearlong story is revealed. It seems that a number of ordinary law-abiding people were trying to live decent peaceful lives in their homes at High View, Ushaw Moor but were being prevented from doing so by drunken yobs who were in the habit of causing a nuisance on a small piece of land behind the houses. The residents put their heads together and came up with an ideal solution, which was to fence off the land. Their first step was to contact the Highways Department, in the person of a lady named Sarah Payne, for advice on the correct procedure because this particular piece of land was occasionally used for access.

The procedure was obtained and followed. Signatures of residents were obtained, notices posted, letters to police, utilities, parish council and post office sent. No objections. Just as the residents were putting the final touches to their plan for a celebratory Road Closing Party, along came Parish Councillor Billy Dousey looking crestfallen. Sorry, there had been a change of plan. You cannot close the path, and if you try to do so the air will be black with lawyers for months, he warned. Fines of up to £1,000 and infinite amounts of court costs await you if you persist in this foolish course of action.

"Hang on, wait a minute, the Parish Council said we could close the path" the residents protested.

"Sorry, but there's been a meeting down at the Labour Group, " the parish councillor explained "and **** ***** says there'll be a lot of trouble if you close that path."

"What, the same **** ***** who was involved in that bother in the men's toilets?" the residents asked.

"Now there was never anything proved about that" the Pparish Ccouncillor protested. "Anyway, **** and Phil Stoddard down at the City say you can't do it, and they'll
do anything they can to stop you if you try."

At this point the dispute escalates, dozens of letters are written and inspectors inspect the small piece of path in question. Letters flew backwards and forwards from the Department of the Environment, Farming and Rural Affairs (DEFRA) in an attempt to find out about the situation. Eventually DEFRA recommended that the path be closed immediately on the grounds that it was unsafe and if any member of the public stumbled and fell, potentially astronomic legal damages could ensue. The overjoyed residents celebrated and fenced off the path.

All seemed well until 20th December 2002 when the residents were visited by County Council solicitor Claudia Freeman, who insisted that the fences must be removed. She appeared completely unphased when shown letters from DEFRA saying that the path must be closed. The path must be reopened as soon as possible, and to avoid astronomic legal damages if any member of the public should stumble on the irregular surface the surface should be made regular at the residents' own expense as soon as possible.

Some time later a letter arrived from DEFRA confirming that they agreed with Ms Freeman's viewpoint and the path must be reopened. They gave no indication as to why they had changed their mind,; indeed it seems as if they were not prepared to accept that they had initially recommended that the path be closed in the first place, despite being shown their own letters to that effect. The residents were bombarded with Durham County Council letters warning them of the dire consequences if they failed to reopen the path. The residents attempted to get the County Council to make the path part of their road plan, which would have meant that the County Council would be responsible for the upgrade and maintenance, but to no effect.

At the moment the situation is at a stalemate and the matter has been referred to at least one ombudsman. That, ladies and gentlemen is a Typical Council Cock-Up of the sort that happens every day. As I am about to leave a news article is thrust into my hand. It is entitled "Criticism for Council over decision to close footpath" Northern Echo, 20th January 2002. "A government watchdog has criticised Durham City Council for abandoning a pledge to reopen a path it illegally closed. Local government Ombudsman Patricia Thomas found the authority guilty of maladministration causing injustice to disabled pensioner Derek Hardman, 61, of Lowland Road, Brandon, who used the path regularly."

I skip through the document, looking for The Usual Suspects. Here we are. "Council Chief Executive Colin Shearsmith guaranteed to reopen and improve the path and pay the complainant £400" Out of his own pocket? Not likely. Out of council tax payers' money of course. "The ombudsman says a report to the Environmental Committee, on which the decision was based, had shortcomings that led to an ill-informed debate by the committee" What, Mr Shearsmith producing a report that mislead a council committee. Surely not?
It goes on "Perhaps more seriously, throughout this affair there have been worrying signs of bias or potential bias in favour of.....two former council officer residents. These included the officer who first closed the path failing to disqualify himself from dealing with the matter despite his close acquaintanceship with Mr B" (the other council officer)

"There was also criticism of the secretive way the closure was carried out and the decision of Chief Executive Colin Shearsmith to meet the two former officers, but not Mr Hardman on site and his acceptance "unquestioningly" of their version of events while "dismissing" Mr Hardman's information."

Surely this cannot be the Colin Shearsmith we all know, and who is so widely respected for his honesty, integrity and hard work throughout the length and breadth of Durham City? "Bias" "Secretive" "Serious maladministration" This has surely got to be some other Durham City Council Chief Executive Colin Shearsmith. Just wait a minute, though, I remember the time when, oh, it must have been the late 1990's……………………

The scene fades to the Cobbler's shop. As I remember it, it happened something like this……..

"If I ran my shop the way that Durham City Council runs Durham, I'd be bankrupt within weeks" the Cobbler thought to himself. In his shop just down and across from the Labour Club in Claypath, Durham City, the Cobbler stood hammering at shoes as he usually did, but today his mind was not really on the job. He knew just about everything there was to know about mending shoes and he knew as much as necessary about running a small business, but the goings-on that had been reported to him since he started publishing newspaper articles about council corruption in his window made no sense. He turned the facts over and over in his mind as he hammered and glued.

****** ********* from Claypath, who used to work with City Council Chief Executive Colin Shearsmith, had just brought the Cobbler a mass of information about a land deal that affected her shop. The Council were planning to sell five shops and council offices, a car park at the bottom of South Street opposite the old Library and recently redecorated premises known as Ruth First House which was a workplace for somewhere between twenty and forty council staff. They then planned to move these staff over to newly constructed offices within the Prince Bishops complex at an extra cost to the taxpayer of about £100,000. ****** had offered to buy the Claypath shop premises, one of the five up for sale, for around £90,000 but was taken aback when her offer was refused. When she asked the reason for the refusal she was told that the five shops could only be bought together as a job lot. No reason for this unusual requirement was forthcoming, and it is alleged that there were other offers, greater than Fulton's, which were turned down.

As an ex-employee this lady was well aware of Shearsmith's deviousness. In the

74

latter stages of her employment with the Council she had found out that a visit by Bishop Desmond Tutu to Durham on a fact-finding mission at a cost reported to be about £15,000. The truth is that it cost the taxpayer almost seven times that much with all of the extra luxuries the Councillors added in for themselves. The difference had been covered up by all manner of creative accountancy techniques and this lady had come to suspect that this was simply the tip of an enormous financial iceberg of conspiracy within the Council offices. As time went on events proved just how right she was.

Over and over again the same names seem to crop up in our story of financial misdemeanour, and first and foremost of The Usual Suspects is a gentleman named Robert Fulton, whose sister-in-law just happened to be City Council Deputy Leader Mildred Brown. Fulton seems to have made his first million from a bus company running out of Langley Park and has never looked back since. Part of the reason for his success would seem to be the fact that he has had a lot of luck in his financial dealings with Durham City Council, and this seems to be the case here. Private Eye articles allege that Fulton and Shearsmith often met on social occasions, including a tennis foursome with Gerry Steinberg MP, and it is possible that Colin Shearsmith may have inadvertently mentioned that a few bargains might be coming up in the near future and that a little bit of capital investment on the part of Fulton would reap rewards in the not-too-distant future.

It was the job of Peter Broome, Head of City Council Legal Services to acquire the Claypath Road Car Park for the Millennium Development which by now Fulton had fortuitously acquired thanks to information from Shearsmith. For reasons never made public, the Council did not put a Compulsory Purchase Order on this valuable piece of land, instead preferring to bargain with Fulton. In return for the car park and £375,000 Fulton received all five properties and Ruth First House. Ruth First House alone is now valued in the region of two million pounds only four years later. As my American colleagues are fond of saying, "Go figure!"

A number of local property developers who heard about this transaction asked to be put on the City Council's Mailing List for Outrageously Profitable Land Deals. When told that no such list was available a great deal of wailing and gnashing of teeth took place and the facts placed before the District Auditor. The District Auditor seems to have looked briefly at the facts, turned two blind eyes and said that nothing was wrong. When dissatisfaction was expressed about this decision the District Auditor suggested that the matter be referred to the Local Government Ombudsman, who promptly claimed that it was nothing to do with him and referred it back to the District Auditor. This is a pass-the-parcel scenario that seems to occur all the time - see the chapter entitled "Anatomy of a Stitch-Up"

The auditors' report about this business is a masterpiece of double-speak. David Parkin, the District Auditor who prepared the report in December 2000 bends so far backwards to find nothing wrong that my back muscles twitch in sympathy as I read his report. It really does make you wonder what these people are paid for. It begins by saying that "The auditor's prime consideration is the stewardship of public funds" - in other words he is there to make sure that public money is spent properly - and then goes on to whitewash the fact that, by his own admission, hundreds of thousands of pounds have been wasted. The report relies heavily on the fact that the police have already investigated the matter and found nothing wrong - wow, that's a relief, folks - mentions his own independent investigation, but does not tell us what he found out, and repeats over and over again that despite the apparently damning evidence nothing has been done that is wrong.

To save the readers from having to look at this sort of stuff themselves (because if you have nothing better to do with your spare time than read auditors; reports I suggest you put this book down and give some serious thought as to how you can reinvigorate your social life) I will summarise his findings:

> Mr Parkin, according to his statutory duties, had looked into the whole thing carefully and concluded **nobody had done anything wrong.**

> He had liaised with the police, who had looked into the whole thing carefully and concluded **nobody had done anything wrong.**

> Despite the fact that Robert Fulton paid £300,000 for a strip of land and some valuable central Durham real estate and in less than two years he sold the land to the Council for £450,000. He still owns the real estate and it is worth its weight in gold, taxpayers paid through the nose, **but Mr Parkin said nobody had done anything wrong**.

> The negotiations for this deal took place almost exclusively between Robert Fulton and Council CEO Colin Shearsmith with nobody else present, and the records of these meetings are minimal. The report is quite cagey about the previous relationship between these two, stating only "The Chief Executive, through his previous role as Head of Economic Development, was aware of Mr Fulton's interest in acquiring city centre properties" but leaves the details of the investigation of this relationship to the police. Elected Councillors were kept completely in the dark about the

whole thing. Shearsmith was also criticised for this sort of secretiveness over Brendan Quayle's film contract, **but Mr Parkin said nobody had done anything wrong.**

In 1997 and again in 1998 the Council was given the opportunity to buy the land for a lot less than it eventually paid for it, knowing that it would be needed in the future. The Council failed to buy it and that decision cost the taxpayer hundreds of thousands of pounds, **but Mr Parkin said nobody had done anything wrong.**

It should have been possible to explore alternatives, and right up until January 1998 there was the possibility that the ransom strip would not be needed, but after that date decisions were made which were irrevocable. There was little or no attempt to bypass the ransom strip, **but Mr Parkin said nobody had done anything wrong.**

After January 1998 it became apparent that Fulton would almost certainly charge an arm and a leg for his land and a various options became available, one of which was a Compulsory Purchase Order. That option was dismissed because it was now too late! Once again there had been a lack of foresight, **but Mr Parkin said nobody had done anything wrong.**

Once it became apparent that there was a massive financial problem the Council's Finance Director should have been called in to evaluate the options, and indeed an officer of the Finance Department sat on the project development team for this purpose, but it did not happen. The Council seemed hell-bent on buying the land from Fulton no matter what he charged, **but Mr Parkin said nobody had done anything wrong.**

That is a typical auditor's report for you. It has only recently come to light that the whole development only extended one metre into the ransom strip. **Moving the development three feet in the opposite direction could have saved the taxpayer millions, apparently. Was this considered? - I rest my case.**

As you can imagine, there was a great deal of concern about this report. Mr Parkin suggested that the matter be referred to the Local Government Ombudsman, who promptly claimed that it was nothing to do with him and referred it back to the District Auditor. This is a pass-the-parcel scenario that seems to occur all the time, and if you look at the chapter entitled "Anatomy of a Stitch-Up" you can see some of the techniques used to frustrate investigations of wrongdoing of this sort. Councillors bear the public brunt of the criticism in matters like this, but they are capable of justifying their actions by calling on the opinions of an impenetrable phalanx of non-accountable auditors, valuers, and god-only-knows what else when necessary.

Eventually Lyn Hunt of the District Auditors office reviewed the facts and once again decided that nothing was wrong. Not satisfied with this a senior City Councillor took a file of documents to the police in the person of Chief Superintendant Suddes. **Within two days the file was returned, saying that the police had investigated the matter and had found nothing wrong. Subsequent investigation showed that Chief Superintendent Suddes had consulted nobody else before making his decision, and the complaint had never been logged.**

At this point the Cobbler was given the information and it ended up in his infamous window. The press got hold of it and soon it became obvious that a scandal of national proportions was in the making. Inspector Pledger of the Fraud Squad was called in to take charge of the matter. and before long an officer named Dave Moralee was knocking on the door of Colin Shearsmith's house. A dark triangle of moisture traversed its way down the leg of Shearsmith's dressing gown as he was being read his rights prior to his arrest. "I've just been in the shower" Shearsmith muttered embarrassedly as he mopped up the steaming pool around his slippers. Despite his protests that he would stop the whole Millennium Development immediately, he was whisked off to Durham Police Station and interrogated.

Gerry Steinberg's constituents would have been gratified if they had seen the effort their MP made to help his tennis partner out of his trouble. More strings seem to have been pulled than all the TV episodes of Thunderbirds put together and in a very short time It was alleged that a senior Labour politician appeared in the office of the Chief Constable, remonstrating with him about the injustice of the whole affair. By all accounts this gentleman himself almost landed in the cells as his demands for action became louder and more frantic. Only threats of arrest for breach of the peace calmed him down. The dispute between Steinberg and the Cobbler, which took place in the middle of the road and stopped the traffic going through the traffic lights, escalated into a four-letter word slanging match that ended up in the pages of Private eye and New Statesman.

"Bumptious" Steinberg was in a particularly foul mood that day, as the Cobbler remembers it. Tony had stepped out of his shop for a bacon sandwich, and was confronted by Steinberg as he thundered up Claypath. "Any more arrests, Gerry?" he shouted across the road to him. The MP turned and bellowed "You're a f*cking *rsehole!" much to the alarm of four elderly ladies who almost suffered neck whiplash as they spun round to the source of this very politically incorrect statement.

"Shut your mouth, Steinberg!" the Cobbler responded, walking determinedly towards him. "How dare you use language like that in front of my readers."

"You're an *rsehole, a f*cking *rsehole" Steinberg repeated over and over again, his eyes bulging out of his head in anger. The Cobbler sensed that Steinberg was close to lashing out at him and put his hands behind his back.

"Are you going to do anything to clean this corruption up?" the Cobbler yelled.

"You're an *rsehole, a f*cking *rsehole" the MP repeated, as he was dragged away by his secretary on the pretext that an important phone call was waiting. The crowd, which had grown alarmingly over the few minutes of the argument, appeared devastated by the un-parliamentary language of their parliamentary representative. Tony Blair was not at all amused when he heard about the antics of "this idiosyncratic MP" and perhaps as a result Steinberg probably lost his position as Chair of the Commons Education Committee. The likelihood is that Blair was even less amused when he heard about Steinberg's embarrassing challenge to ex-Conservative Leader William Hague in the Commons tearoom after the vote on Foundation Hospitals.

The story, as it appeared in the Sunday newspapers, suggests that Steinberg, full of himself after the Labour victory, tried to reserve a whole table for himself and his colleagues. Hague and company arrived .and sat down at this table, and was immediately challenged. "That's wor table" Gerry claimed, reverting to the assumed Geordie accent he normally reserved for the working men's clubs of his constituency. "If yu touch it, I'll take ya outside and giya the biggest hidin' u yu life!"

"Come on then Gerry, or have you forgotten I'm a judo black-belt?" Haigue responded.

Steinberg's jowls wobbled. He knew that Hague was a fellow bullshit merchant, but he really was a black belt. "OK, have the table" he scowled and retreated to another table. Hague smiled because he knew that he may have lost the battle for

Foundation Hospitals, but the battle of the tables was his. Sorry for that diversion, dear reader, this sad humiliation of the Geordie fighting spirit took place in late 2003 and the story I am trying to tell you happened in Summer 2001, but it's such a good story I could not resist telling it to you here. Anyway, back to the Rottenest Borough in England, aka Durham City 2001 in your imagination if you please.

By this time Inspector Pledger had the bit between his teeth and the investigation moved forward apace. "However bad you think the situation to be" he advised the Cobbler "the reality is twenty times worse." Meantime in the background strings were being tugged very hard and you cannot pull that many strings without something moving. In fact from what I can see just about everybody seems to have moved elsewhere. Despite his protests and very much against his will, Dave Morillee was taken off the case and moved onto the stolen car squad, a definite career downturn for any ambitious officer. Inspector Pledger took early retirement, and Lyn Hunt either took a year's sabbatical or a year away with health problems depending upon which version of the story you read, and Peter Broome applied for early retirement. A new team was drafted in, each one equipped with a whitewash brush.

Meanwhile, after seven months on bail, Shearsmith and Fulton were informed that the charges against them had been dropped for lack of evidence. Anthony Barry of the York Crown Prosecution Service was asked for clarification of the decision, but remains unavailable for comment right up to this day. Whether or not they were aware that Inspector Suddes refused to log the complaint and investigated the matter by himself in less than two working days we will never know because he has also moved to the district only known as "Elsewhere"

If you think that this is just history and there is no point raking over it then consider these facts which are a matter of public record. On 24th June 2002 a house that had previously been council property at 16 Winney Hill, close to Durham Prison, was sold for £67,000 to Hope Estates Ltd of Davis Burton Selleck, Old Boundry House, London Road, Sunningdale, Ascot. The Durham Land Registry title number is DU253353, so you can check this information for yourself. The sale of the property was not advertised locally and the local Right To Buy regulations appear to have been ignored. **The names on the documentation associated with the sale were Durham City Mayor Eilleen Rochford (one of the four people who contested the Labour nomination for City of Durham Member of Parliament) and City Council Solicitor Leslieey Blackie.**

At about the same time that this sale took place, a sitting tenant enquired about buying an identical property after renting it for about three years, by exercising his Right To Buy. The price quoted was £150,000 after a 25% discount, which he could not afford. Because of the spiralling house prices in central Durham City by October 2003 similar properties in the area were valued at about £230,000. It would seem therefore that somebody has been given a bargain by the City Council and that approximately £100,000, which could have gone into the funds of Durham City Council to help relieve the spiralling Council Tax increases, did not do so. Instead they went to an anonymous buyer in London.

The most worrying part of this is the fact that there is absolutely no way for an ordinary person to find out whether this is a one-off incident or just one of a series of similar transactions because the cloak of secrecy continues to cover up deals of this sort, thanks to the devious legal skills of City Council Solicitor Leslie Blackie. This one-off incident pales into insignificance however when you hear about scams such as the Ushaw Moor playing field scam.

Nationally one of the biggest Labour Party scandals which has come to light in recent years was the Doncaster Council property development scandal involving a company by the name of Keepmoat, that became so notorious it eventually came to be known as "Donnygate". John Burton, Tony Blair's electoral agent gets very upset when you mention Donnygate because a number of Labour councillors were involved and it brought very considerable disrepute upon the party. You would have thought that the Labour Party would have learnt some sort of lesson, but no. Now read on.

In 1922 Broome Parish Council borrowed £900 from the Ministry of Health to buy a beautiful piece of land in scenic Deerness Valley as a recreation ground, and it was stated quite specifically in the deeds that this land was to be used "for recreational purposes". It was divided up into various parts including a cricket pitch, a football pitch and a children's play park. In 1974 Durham City Council took over the maintenance of the area, such as cutting the grass. Gradually it fell into disrepair until eventually it became so run down it was closed because it was deemed to be unsafe for use. Some cynical local councillors say that it was deliberately starved of funds so that it would become unsafe, and this explanation certainly fits the pattern.

It came to the attention of the people of Ushaw Moor that Durham City Council planned to donate this land for redevelopment to a building company known as Haslam Homes. The residents of Ushaw Moor were up in arms because they had the title deeds saying quite clearly that this was public land, not the property of

Durham City Council. The residents tried for two years to get Durham County Council to verify the registration of the land as public property and for recreational use only. Durham County Council did a brief investigation and declared that because the City Council had maintained it, it was now the property of Durham City Council to dispose of as they saw fit. Furthermore, since the playground was derelict it was no longer a green-field site, it was derelict land and therefore suitable for redevelopment as building land. The residents became suspicious and sought a Public Inquiry into the whole development, which opened in October 2001.

I am not an expert on the process but the basis of the planning system, as I understand it, is that a Council draws up a Local Plan which allocates land for certain use. If it is questioned then that plan is tested at a Public Inquiry by an independent inspector who recommends whether or not the proposed allocations should become an adopted policy. Durham City Council was so desperate to develop the open land at Ushaw Moor that it granted planning permission before the inspector, Mr John Shepherd, had decided whether or not the land should be allocated for development. The infamous Planning Permission Committee of Durham City Council granted themselves planning permission to build upon the land **which was donated, not sold, to Haslam Homes because it was of no use to the Council itself**, being derelict land, and **the development went ahead in May 2002 without waiting for the results of the Public Inquiry**. Four months later, in August 2002 John Shepherd produced his report on the results of the Public Inquiry, **finding for the people of Ushaw Moor and against the City Council**, on the basis that there was insufficient evidence to support the development. **Too late, because planning permission had already been granted by the City Council and the Haslam Homes development was already at the advanced planning stage.**

Faced with the prospect of a costly legal battle against Haslam Homes and the City Council, the residents gave up the struggle. Building work started in May 2003. I was up there today, 19th October 2003 to look at the site. With its beautiful rural outlook and close proximity to historic Durham City you can expect some very nice and no doubt very expensive executive houses to be there soon. There is a big notice board right next to the development saying **"Haslam Homes, a subsidiary of Keepmoat PLC"**

City Council leader Maurice Crathorne, his associate John Bowman, and City Council Officer Brian Spears (now Durham's Chief Executive) all went on holiday from Newcastle to Spain for an alleged all-expenses-paid holiday in a luxurious villa in Spain, paid for by a local property developer. Spears admitted this to the Cobbler in February 2004, justifying his actions by saying that he had paid for it with his own credit card. Nevertheless, where is the distance that is supposed to be maintained between council members and the officers who serve them? On the face of this, it appears, at the very least, to be highly unethical. Maurice Crathorne likes nothing better than a day at the races, and can be seen quite frequently at Doncaster Racecourse. He has some wealthy and influential friends there.

You do not have to dig very deep before you find that the same people who were involved in Donnygate are also involved in shady property dealings in and around Durham, Doncaster, Sheffield and Hull. Historians of scandals of this sort will prick up their ears at the name of Newcastle Council boss T Dan Smith who set up an "industrialised building firm" called Open System Building in 1964. In 1966 this was taken over by the infamous John Poulson. Later this resurfaced as a contractor building houses in Pontefract using as an agent Haslam Homes, which is of course a subsidiary of Keepmoat. This massive spider's web of interlocking building companies seems to have only one big spider in the middle, and more arrests in Doncaster may be imminant. Watch this space, because this may yet blow up into a massive scandal

In Durham the distinction between publicly and privately owned housing has blurred over the years until there is no real distinction anymore. In 1995 a joint venture company was set up entitled Durham Housing Association (DHP)with Keepmoat owning 81% of the shares and Durham City Council owning 19%. Why these odd numbers you may be asking? The answer is simple. If the council owned 20% then there would have to be public access to the records, and that would not go down well with Keepmoat. Maurice Crathorne is the City's director on the DHP board and the supposedly independent "community directors" are Colin Ord and Fred Burn, both Labour members and friends of Crathorne.

Just to finish this story, here is a direct quote from Jim Hackett "I believe that both Durham County Council and Durham City Council's idea of a green belt is a leather strap worn around the waists of Robin Hood and his Merry Men to stop their tights from falling around their ankles and showing what arseholes they really are". The County Council are to sell off (or dispose of) a playing field at Esh Winning, two and a half miles from Ushaw Moor, and The Duffy in Gilesgate, which was also public land was sold off for a paltry £7,000, allegedly. A sizeable development now stands there.

Update February 8th 2004

I have in front of me a document entitled " Durham Housing Partnership - Proposed

Phase 2 Sites. Not For Publication" Wrong - here it is. It gives details of land already sold and getting ready to be sold. Could this have been part of the mysterious missing treasurer's report from the last full council meeting under Labour? Here are the rest.

DURHAM HOUSING PARTNERSHIP
PROPOSED PHASE 2 SITES

	Site Name	Sale	Type	Rented	Type	Housing Association
Year 1						
1	Former Depot & Frontage, Gilesgate	49	2/3/4br house	21	2br bungalows	DAMHA *
2	Former Depot, Sherburn Village	-	-	8	2br bungalows	TRHA
3	Landsdowne Road, Coxhoe	-	-	9	2br bungalows	DAMHA *
4	Broomside Lane, Carrville	-	-	5	2br bungalows	TRHA
5	Pinders Way, Sherburn Hill	41	2/3/4br house	-	-	-
6	Woodbine Road, Pity Me	24	2/3br house	-	-	-
Year 2						
7	Finchale Road, Framwellgate Moor	-	-	18	2br bungalows	DAMHA *
8	Kepier Crescent, Gilesgate Moor	-	-	25	15 2br bungalows	DAMHA *
					10 3br houses	TRHA
9	Cook Avenue, Bearpark	-	-	9	2br bungalows	TRHA
10	Lund Avenue, Framwellgate Moor	-	-	9	2br bungalows	TRHA
11	Woodside, Shadforth	12	2/3br house	6	2 2br bungalows	TRHA
					4 3br houses	
12	Louisa Terrace, Witton Gilbert	12	2/3/4br house	-	-	-
		138		110		

In case the reader thinks that this sort of thing only happens with the Labour Party, the LibDems may be responsible for the sale of Sherburn Depot, which had a lot of money spent on it only two years ago. It was sold off without going out to tender, as usual. Guess who it was sold off to? Yes, you've got it in one - **Haslem Homes.**

Similar arrangements are in place with Durham Aged Mineworkers Association, whose chairman just happens to be one of Maurice's many relatives within council schemes, in this case his brother Alan. The other large housing association in Durham, Three Rivers Housing Association is also controlled by Labour place-men (or should it be place-persons?) As in Ushaw Moor, public land is transformed by some mysterious alchemy on the behalf of the Planning Permission Committee from green field to brown field, and then developed by Keepmoat or one of its subsidiaries. It is then built upon but only one third of the housing stock that results

84

is kept for public use and the rest goes to Keepmoat. All over Durham valuable public land is disappearing and valuable private houses are appearing, courtesy of the activities of the stalwarts of City of Durham Constituency Labour Party. The amount of money that Durham City taxpayers see in return is negligible. Similar schemes are going on in Hull and Doncaster, and probably all over the place for all we know.

We all got a sense of deja-vu on November 15th 2003 when the same thing seemed to be happening all over again in Nevilles Cross. HJ Banks are a building firm that are redeveloping the New College Durham site for executive housing and offices and part of the council-approved development plan calls for a substantial part of that land to remain as green field recreational land. "Splendid idea" says Tom Shanks, Professor of Astronomy at Durham University. "Let's register it as public land so that no matter how much its value increases in the future it cannot be built upon. After all, it has been used by the people of Durham City for recreational purposes for more than forty years."

"Not so" says Andrew North, Professor of Ambiguity at Durham County Council's Legal Department. "For part of this time it has been used as a rugby pitch by students, so that constitutes a change of use during the mandatory twenty year period, therefore the land should not be registered as public land." Come on Andrew, that is not fair. Students are people too, are they not? OK, maybe not law students, but apart from them it is obvious that students are simply other people's boys and girls who are living away from home for a while, and want to roll about on the grass and get dirty once a week during term time for recreational purposes, as normal young people frequently do. "Sorry". " says Mr North "We reserve the right for it to be sold off at some time in the future and buildt on." The rest of the County Council agree with him, so that appears to be the end of the story.

That is a fairly typical story of how your councils turn public land into private profit. Of course every now and again uncomfortable details about the suspicious activities of councillors come to light, and damaging publicity results. Anxious to make sure that a similar scandal to Donnygate never happens again, New Labour has developed an overlapping armour of non-accountability to protect itself. Council officers are accountable to the elected councillors. Councillors themselves are accountable only to a new organisation known as the Standards Board of England, run under the auspices of the Office of the Deputy Prime Minister John Prescott.

The Standards Board will not investigate anything that occurred before mid-2002, so any misdemeanours before that time cannot be investigated and to all intents and purposes they have been forgiven. For matters relating to allegations after that time the Standards Board has the power to reject any or all allegations against councillors without giving detailed reason for their adjudication, and without appeal other than going to a court of law. This is an impossibly difficult and expensive task for the ordinary citizen, because Tony Blair has made it very much more difficult to obtain legal aid for this sort of case.

In the wake of the September 11th attacks Tony Blair took on a raft of powers to cover up the workings of politicians, ostensibly under the guise of Prevention of Terrorism. If he decides that it is not in the interest of the public to know a certain piece of information he has the power to prevent the publication of that information for up to 100 years, on pain of criminal charges. This is known as the D-notice system. Faced with the knowledge that if they choose to challenge the government and publish an awkward piece of information it will be suppressed by the D-notice system, most editors simply self-regulate and do not attempt to push the boundaries. Greg Pallast's chapter entitled "Kissing the Whip" in his book "The Best Democracy Money Can Buy" is excellent reading if you want to learn more about this sort of thing.

At a local level the minutes of the meetings of Durham City Council are available at the little office that is situated right next to the public toilets in the Town Hall if you are interested. Apparently the local press are not, because the people in that little office tell me that no local reporters have bothered to pick them up for years now. The only real contact the average citizen has with the workings of the Council is the time when the Council Tax demand drops through their letterbox. The spiralling cost of this tax has reached, in the words of the government itself "the limits of acceptability." There are those on low fixed incomes who say that it has already exceeded that limit and are prepared to go to prison in a wave of civil disobedience that is likely to equal that of Thatcher's downfall, the Poll Tax.

Overall there is no way that the ordinary citizen can ever find out whether their money is being spent wisely or not, and it is my belief that this is the way that the government wants it to be. They say that they want the very best people in local politics and the way to recruit them is to make sure that politics is a well paid job. If local politicians are supplementing their incomes locally with a few shady deals then it seems likely that the only message from 10 Downing Street is likely to be a knowing wink. The adage "as above, so below" springs immediately to mind.

Chapter 7
James

Even on the highest throne we are seated still on our arses.

Montaigne

The borderline between comedy and tragedy is wafer-thin at times. That was my immediate thought when Tthe Cobbler told me the story of James.

Durham is a city of wide contrasts. At the very top of the booming property market is Quarryheads Lane, just north of the Science Site of Durham University. The owners of these opulent houses enjoy the anonymity afforded by their long leafy drives and high fences, but past and present residents include John Marshall, owner of the Durham Pine furniture company who sold his house to build an even bigger one overlooking the cricket field and Mike Weston, a wonderfully modest ex-international rugby star and partner in the ubiquitous Close & Weston estate agents.

There are three schools leading off Quarryheads Lane, all of them open to those who can afford the fees. At the very top of the ladder of prestige are the grey-and-purple-blazered boys and girls of Chorister School, nestling next to the Cathedral. This exclusive preparatory school has been at this site for hundreds of years and enjoys its reputation of high achievement in both academic and musical studies. State school parents dote over their children's Christmas Nativity play while Choristers rehearse Faure's Requiem in the Cathedral. You need brains as well as money to get into Choristers, and this school was the choice of Alderman Blair for his son Tony.

If your idea of a good education for a little boy is to dress him in short trousers and keep him away from little girls for as long as possible (not a bad idea actually), you might want to send him to the equally prestigious Bow School, whose beautiful leafy green playground lies next door to the Durham University Science Library. I suppose that a book like this should be condemning elitist organisations such as Bow and Choristers, but the fact is that these schools provide the sort of education that every right-minded parent would want for their child. If Blair was serious about "Education, education, education" being his three main priorities then he would be trying to make state schools more like Bow and Choristers where children actually enjoy their education, and less like the pile-them-deep, teach-them-cheap stress factories most children are forced to attend.

There are a number of acquaintances of mine who teach in state schools so that they can afford to send their children to one or other of these two fee-paying schools and that has got to be the highest accolade possible. Both schools feed a high proportion of their youngsters into Durham School, a fee-paying senior school just a little further along the road. As well as those who scrimp and save for an education a lot of the parents of pupils of these schools are rich - not ordinary rich but really rich. Throwing-away-money rich, as one ex-member of staff described it to me. A famous ex-pupil of one of these schools was the grandson of a wealthy local property developer who also invested heavily in a local football club, she told me.

The story goes that one day this little boy had committed some minor offence, and was being reprimanded in his headmaster's office. Eventually the humiliation of this proved too much for him, and he lifted his gaze up from the carpet, fixing his headteacher firmly in the gaze of his bright little eyes.

"You'd better be careful what you say to me, or my granddad will buy this school, sack you and redevelop it as housing estate!"

By all accounts the headteacher stared at him for a moment, considered his position carefully and then sent the small boy back to his classroom.

When they grow a little older these boys and girls might move just down the road to Durham University, which is esteemed only slightly less than Oxford and Cambridge by those who care about that sort of thing. The wealthier Durham students are nicknamed The Rahs by their less well-off colleagues, because of their cries of "Oh, Hoo-Rah-Well-Darn!" that ring out from Baths Bridge on boat-race days. High point of the Rah season is the Midsummer Ball at Durham Castle when at dawn the grass on the forecourt is black with young men in evening dress, draining the last drops of champagne from their bottles before jumping into their sports cars on their way home to a well-earned day's sleep.

A couple of miles away but right at the other end of the social spectrum you will find Sherburn Road Estate, one of the most deprived areas in Western Europe. Think of the movie Trainspotting in a Geordie accent, take away Ewan McGregor and all of the funny bits, replace them with chronic unemployment, hopelessness and abject despair, courtesy of Margaret Thatcher and the 1983 miners' strike, and you have the flavour of life in Sherburn Road Estate.

Poverty, misery, drug-addiction and mental illness have always gone hand-in-hand, and Sherburn Road Estate is no exception. Most of the people there are good honest people who are trying to earn a living and bring up children in an area where there are simply no jobs for them to go to. Teenagers are bombarded with advertising that tells them they are not worthwhile individuals unless they are wearing a pair of £100 trainers on their feet, while their parents have less than that to feed and house a family of five for a week. Crime becomes the only road to respectability and reality turns upside down for these young people. Parents sink into a state of chronic depression without even daring to admit it even to themselves, because of the fear of the stigma of mental illness in an area where the only thing to be is rock-f*cking-hard.

In his shop two miles away, Tthe Cobbler warmed his twentieth stick-on sole of the day over the small electric fire on the workbench. By now he had worked out that there were four sorts of people who came into his shop. First and foremost there were the people who wanted to have their shoes repaired, and then there were the Council whistleblowers who supplied the information that covered the inside of his infamous shop window. Next came the ones who wanted to moan and bitch about the world in general and Durham City Council in particular. Finally there were the lonely ones who had nobody else to talk to.

The young man standing in front of him, with a grin on his face and a long black nylon wig on his head did not fit readily into any of these categories, The Cobbler thought to himself. Either a nutter or a student - it's often difficult to tell the difference. The young man opened his mouth, and a long string of unintelligible words came out.

"Definitely a student" Tony thought to himself.

"Behold, I am Blackula. God has caused me to disengage from The Matrix to help you in your struggle against the forces of oppression that seek to destroy you and those like you. We are both His freedom fighters"

"Pardon?" said the bemused Cobbler

"Do not be afraid, I mean you no harm. I simply wish to guide you, to show you how to disconnect yourself from The Matrix. God has called you towards your first step on the path to enlightenment. I am not Him, I am simply his messenger, I am here to help you, but we must act quickly before they find me and force me to go back. There is very little time"

"Look, I'm very sorry, but I'm really busy. If this is some sort of student thing, can you come back some other time?" the Cobbler said, without pausing from his hammering.

"There is no time to waste, we have a task of the utmost importance. Please come with me now." The young man was becoming agitated, and the hair of the wig slipped over his face. He brushed it back in a way that reminded The Cobbler of a 60's John Lennon.

"This is some sort of Council p*ss-take, isn't it? Well look, I'm really busy. You've had your bit of fun, so get back over to the Labour Club and tell them all about it. OK?"

The face under the black wig appeared hurt. "No, no, you don't understand. Here are my contacts. These are the members of the resistance." He handed The Cobbler a blue hard-backed notebook, which he opened at the first page. His eye fell upon a list of telephone numbers.

"Social   services..........social   worker........psychiatric   outpatient department......" his voice trailed off into realisation. "Look, which one of these do you want me to phone?"

"No, no, please........." The black wig was whirling in agitation by now.

"Hang on, just calm down. There's no need to get upset. Are you hungry, can I get you a Mars Bar or something like that?" The black-wigged figure was pacing around the shop, mumbling words in a voice too low to hear. Tony picked up the mobile phone that he kept on the shelf next to the counter and dialled the first number on the list. The phone rang for a moment.

"Hello, this is Durham Social Services. I am sorry there is nobody to take your call at the moment, but......" Next number.

"Hello, this is Durham Psychiatric Outpatient. This department is closed at present. If.........." One by one The Cobbler worked his way down the list. Nothing - it was 5.30 on a winter Friday evening and the world of psychiatry was closed for the weekend. There was nothing else for it, The Cobbler dialled the last number on the list - Durham Police.

"Hello, it's Tony Martin from the Cobbler's Shop."
"Just hang on for a moment, Mr Martin. I'll put you on to the Desk Sergeant."

"Hello Mr Martin." The Desk Sergeant's voice was heavy with tired resignation. "What are you complaining about today?"

"I've got this guy in my shop. He's wearing a black wig and he's very upset. I think he's escaped from somewhere, but I can't get anybody to answer the phone."

"OK Mr Martin, I'll send somebody down straight away."

As I listened to my recording of The Cobbler's recorded account of this incident, I could not prevent my thoughts drifting towards what might have taken place in Durham police station just after that Desk Sergeant had put that phone down. Here are two possible scenarios that came to mind immediately. I will leave it to the judgement of the individual reader to decide which is the more likely, bearing in mind that since the illegal surveillance operation the Cobbler's relationship with Durham Constabulary could best be described as "tense."

Scenario 1

The Desk Sergeant is addressing two young constables in Durham Police Station

Desk Sergeant: Right, Lads, it seems that the unfortunate young man in the black wig who temporarily escaped from the psychiatric care facility at our local hospital yesterday is now in The Cobblers Shop in Claypath. I would like you to go up there and investigate the situation immediately.

Constables: Yes, sergeant.

Desk Sergeant: Now, as you are no doubt aware, due to several unfortunate lapses in our normal high standard of service to the public, Mr Martin has been forced to make a number of well-founded complaints that are presently being investigated by the Chief Constable.

Constables: Yes, sergeant.

Desk Sergeant: Now, I want there to be no slip-ups this time, lads. Go up there and make Mr Martin aware of what it is really like to be under the protection of the officers of Durham Constabulary. Off you go now. Remember, lads - make me proud!

Constables: Yes, sergeant! *(Razor-sharp salute)*

Exit Constables. Blue lights flash. Noise of car moving away.

Scenario 2

The Desk Sergeant is addressing two young constables in Durham Police Station

Desk Sergeant: Right, lads. It looks like that nutter in the black wig that escaped from The County yesterday has ended up in The Cobbler's Shop in Claypath.

First Constable: I'm not surprised, Sergeant. You know what they say about like attracting like, eh?

Second Constable: Yeh, they're all up there in that shop of his, them nutters. Flypaper for freaks that guy is, if you ask me.

Desk Sergeant: Right, get up there sharp and haul him in. Be careful, cos you know what nutters are like. If necessary, jarp 'im one to calm him down. If the Cobbler gives you any lip, jarp 'im one as well and the lads'll give him the hard word down in the cells, OK?

Constables: Yes, Sergeant.

Desk Sergeant: Now, the Chief Constable is sick of that Cobbler and his everlasting complaints so get up there sharp and get him sorted. Don't take no lip off him mind, he's got it coming.

Constables: Yes, sergeant! *(Razor-sharp salute)*

Exit Constables. Blue lights flash. Noise of car moving away.

Back to reality. Blue lights flash in the dark winter evening outside the Cobbler's shop, and the situation turns from farce to tragedy in a way that would surprise anyone unfamiliar with the symptoms of severe mental illness. Two young policemen burst through the Cobbler's door, truncheons in their hands. The black wigged figure screams and dives for a corner of the shop counter, curling himself up in the foetal position as if attempting to make himself as small as possible in the desperate hope that they might not see him.

"Right, come along please, we don't want any trouble, do we?" A young policeman attempts to grab the curled-up figure by the shoulder. It screams a high-pitched scream like a strangled rabbit and pulls away, trying to make itself even smaller.

"Right, get hold of him......" The figure rolls away across the floor and the police follow him, trying to get a grip on the tight cloth of the coat.

No.......Please.......No!.........Please...." By now the black wig is upside down on the floor and the terrified owner is sobbing. "Please don't let them take me back, please...."

"Hang on, " said the Cobbler "you'll frighten the bloody life out of him man. Just hang on a minute." He turns to the figure on the floor." Listen, you'll be all right. These lads have come to help you. They have come to take you back to your friends."

"No........." A high-pitched, desperate screech of despair. "No, please.........."

"Listen, listen, ..." The Cobbler is kneeling beside the terrified figure, the policeman watching silently. This goes on for quite some time, and bit by bit the curled up figure starts to unroll like a giant spikeless hedgehog, as it begins to realise that the danger is not quite as bad as it first feared.

"Will you come with me? Please come with me.........Please....."

"Listen, I can't. These lads are here to help you, honest......"

"Please........." The high-pitched insistent note is back in the voice. "Please ....."

"Look, I can't..... There's nobody to look after the shop. These lads are not going to hurt you. Look......." The Cobbler points to the silent policemen beside the door. "Please............" Quieter this time.

"Look, there's nothing to be afraid of, honestly. I'll help you get into the car." The figure gets to its feet, and painfully starts to straighten up. Suddenly it starts to resemble a human being again.

"Please will you look after my book?"

"Yeh, look, I'll bring it to you when you are feeling a bit better. Honestly" Eye contact for the first time since the police arrived. Something is different in the back of the eyes, thought The Cobbler.

By now the young man is through The Cobbler's Shop door and the car doors are open. He leans forward and sits down. No more eye contact, he returns into his own confused world.

"My book......."

"Yes, don't worry, it's here, it's safe....."

"Thanks, mate" one of the policeman says, quietly. Doors slam, they drive off into the night.

For the first time the Cobbler realises his hands are shaking and his palms are sweating. Time to close the shop and go home.

There, lying beside the bits of scrap leather and bent nails is the book. The Cobbler opens it and looks at the pages. Poetry, algebraic formulae and hauntingly beautiful ballpoint-pen sketches are mixed up with page after page of indecipherable scrawl, written at such a pace that the pen hardly had time to touch the paper. The Cobbler closed the book, switched off the lights, locked the shop and headed towards the Tyne Tunnel and home.

The next morning a plump, smiling social worker entered the Cobbler's Shop.

"Thanks for helping James last night. He talked about nothing else last night, you've made a friend there."

"It's alright, I was just pleased to be able to help, you know what I mean?"

"I know exactly what you mean" said the social worker. "He wants his book back, he says you're looking after it for him."

"Yeh, it's here. I've had a look at it, there's some funny stuff in there, mind."

"Oh, yes. He was a clever guy before the breakdown. Headed for a First in Natural Sciences at Cambridge, and then something happened. Things just went wrong, and his parents brought him back. He has his good spells, but most of the time he's with us."

"Does he live around here, then?" asked The Cobbler.

"Yes, said the young social worker, smiling. "He lives in a great big house over the other side of Durham, just off Quarryheads Lane. Lots of money. Well, thanks very much. Bye." She picked up the book, turned and was gone.

"Bye now." said The Cobbler, turning back to the stick-on soles.

He never saw either of them again. The black wig is still in the shop.

Chapter 8
A Law Unto Themselves

The law is like a spider's web. Small, weak things are caught where larger, stronger creatures simply blunder through.

Marcus Aurelius

The Police. The Constabulary. Coppers. The Law. The Bizzis. Pigs. Call them what you like, we all seem to have an ambiguous relationship with the Forces of Law and Order. We hate them when that little envelope drops through the door saying that you have been caught on a speed camera, but it's a different matter when you wake up in the middle of the night and there are strange noises going on downstairs. Who you gonna call, Ghostbusters?

Yes, as the shrewder readers will have already worked out from the available evidence, this chapter is about Durham Constabulary and the legal machinery behind them. Let's get this straight right from the start. It is the opinion of this author, and Tony the Cobbler himself that 99% of the ordinary men and women in Durham Constabulary are honest, hardworking people who are dedicated to the job of making Durham City a better place. The problem is that like most police forces honesty and hard work are by no means the best way to get promotion in the force, and like the rest of us the police are forced to dance to the tune the politicians play.

This is not just my opinion, it is the opinion of lots and lots of police I have talked to, who have spent countless hours studying for various qualifications to improve their promotion prospects, have passed their exams and have found that it has done them no good because there are other barriers that need to be surmounted, and the qualities needed to surmount these are by no means clear cut. There has always been an immense amount of resentment about this, with less- talented officers leapfrogging their better and harder working colleagues, and nothing seems to be happening about it.

The big problem seems to be that if they chose to do so, the senior figures in a police force, such as the Chief Constable, seem to be capable of making themselves completely autonomous, answering to nobody. They are a law unto themselves, as the phrase goes. Tony the Cobbler's relationship with senior Durham police officers had soured considerably since he complained about the illegal police surveillance operation mounted from the office above Gerry Steinberg's office, designed (so he believes) to provide evidence that would have been used to "fit him up" as a drug dealer. Unfortunately things were soon to get a lot worse.

The Cobbler had just lost the County Council election to Peter Thompson in May 2001 and he was not happy about it. It is not just that he was a sore loser, but it seemed that the Labour Party dirty tricks machine had simply steam-rollered him. The Cobbler had been forced to run his campaign on a shoestring (like the pun?) because of lack of funds and the Labour Party had thrown everything they had at him, including a lot of mud, yet despite all of that, the Cobbler had lost by a very narrow margin. You can read all about it in the chapter called "Election Time."

Sitting here at my computer in February 2004, with the Hutton Inquiry controversy in full swing. it seems to me that the population as a whole are only now just beginning to understand how Tony's Cronies deal with those who get in their way, and the massive dive in Blair's popularity is the result. Not before time, many of us in the Labour Party might add, but in May 2001 when Labour had just achieved a second electoral landslide victory, it was very difficult to get any sort of dissenting voice heard and it is still not easy.

In the run-up to the election the Labour Party dirty tricks machine had been working overtime and as a result the Cobbler's reputation was in tatters. He was aggrieved and wanted to complain about it, but where to start? The obvious starting point was to complain to the Labour Party itself. All complaints about the Labour Party ended up on the desk of Chris Lennie who was then in sole charge of Labour North after the mysterious disappearance of his colleague Brian Thistlethwaite from the political scene. I would be grateful if anybody who knows the present whereabouts of Mr Thistlethwaite would contact me via the Cobbler's shop, because his sudden disappearance from local politics led some of us to consider the possibility that he might be "sleeping with the fishes" in North Tyneside harbour somewhere. In the absence of this good and honest man all complaints about Labour Party politicians ended up on the desk of Chris Lennie, and that was the end of the matter.

If you phoned Mr Lennie to ask about your complaint, he was never there. It is clear that this is the way that The Party wanted it because this tactic eventually earned Chris Lennie the post of Assistant General Secretary of the Labour Party, second in hierarchy only to David Triesman, and he was eventually given the job of getting rid of George Galloway MP. By now the Cobbler had come to the conclusion that a reasonable alternative to writing to Chris Lennie was to take the letters, roll them up into a tight ball and stick them where the squirrel hid its nuts. He had lost the County Council election by a narrow margin. Rumours had been spread, both on the internet and on the streets, that the Cobbler had been involved in sex scandals against young boys and this had had an obvious effect on his trade and popularity. He wanted something done about it. His website had been hacked and destroyed, and in its place pictures of young girls performing lesbian sex acts had been displayed.

The culprits were known, they had confessed to the crime and two of them had connections to Durham County Council. One was James Davie, the son of Frazer Davie, Press Officer for Durham County Council and the other was Luke Wilson, son of Shiela Wilson who is now secretary to Council leader Ken Manton. The Cobbler wanted something done about it because all of this was a crime under the Representation of the People Act and that is how the matter came into the jurisdiction of Durham Constabulary.

The procedure is straightforward. You go to the police, make your complaint and they take a statement from you. They investigate and the facts go to the Crown Prosecution Service to see if the case is worth pursuing. The facts were straightforward in that four young men had hacked the Cobbler's guest book from a computer based at Durham Johnston Comprehensive School Upper Site, a Durham County Council school and another attack to his website took place from Frazer Davie's home These young men were responsible for a series of allegations made on the website's guest-book that the Cobbler was molesting children and threats that he would be knee-capped. The cost of repairing the damage to the website had been £900, but the damage to the Cobbler's reputation had been incalculable. It seemed like an open and shut case.

The Cobbler made his statement to the police who said they would type it up and get it back to him. A few days later a policeman came into the Cobbler's shop with the lengthy statement in his hands. The Cobbler started to read it when a customer came in. He stopped reading the statement to attend to the customer and the policeman started making dissatisfied noises about being busy, please just sign the statement because it is just what you told us etc.etc. In his naivety the Cobbler picked up the blue ballpoint pen from his workbench and signed. The policeman thanked him and left.

Soon after that the threatening phone calls started - abusive, violent language threatening him and his family. The Cobbler managed to tape one and passed it on to the police, but the calls still continued. A short while later, the Cobbler's shop was visited by Sgt. Pargeter of Durham Police, who told the Cobbler that it was their intention to caution the boys over the incident. Of course, the Cobbler was dissatisfied and requested that the matter be sent to the Crown Prosecution Service. Eventually Sgt Pargeter agreed and left the shop. A few weeks later he received a letter from the Crown Prosecution Service saying that because of the boys' previously good record it was not in the public interest for the prosecution to go ahead. The final straw was when the Cobbler was told that his own thirteen year-old son, with an equally unblemished record, was to be prosecuted for sitting on a motorbike in a North Tyneside cul-de-sac.

An increasingly heated dialogue was now taking place between the Cobbler and Geoff Corrigan of the Crown Prosecution Service in Durham about why they refused to prosecute the website hackers. Eventually the Cobbler requested to see the information that had gone to the CPS from Durham Constabulary. After another lengthy wait this arrived, and the Cobbler was astounded when he saw the contents of the brown envelope. The statement he had made bore very little resemblance to what had gone to the CPS, with massive omissions in it. The most noticeable change, however, was that the statement now said that he did not want the boys prosecuted!

By now the Gala Theatre scandal was in full swing and after only a couple of weeks staff were being sacked. Several came into the Cobbler's shop telling stories of all sorts of misdeeds, including allegations of drug taking by the management while on the premises and the substitution of cheap own-label spirits from the local Bottoms-Up off licence for the expensive Teachers and Grouse whiskeys in the optics in the bar. A token inspection of the bar was made by Trading Standards people, but nothing was found to be wrong. What a surprise! It was certainly no surprise to the remaining bar staff who had known of the inspection well in advance, and presumably had taken appropriate measures to make sure nothing was amiss. This incident led to another heated conversation, this time between the Cobbler and Prince Bishops manager Peter Benyon.

It is alleged that during this conversation Mr Benyon stated that if allegations of drug-taking by the Prince Bishops management appeared in the Cobblers window **"I will pray for the well-being of your children, Mr Martin."** The Cobbler then told Mr Benyon that he was taping the conversation. Mr Benyon quickly changed his mind, saying **"No, I didn't mean that, I didn't mean to threaten your children."** I can only leave that to the judgment of the individual reader as to whether a statement like that would normally be interpreted as a threat to the Cobbler's family or simply the pious utterings of a deeply religious man. The police, who were subsequently informed of the conversation, appeared to interpret it as the latter. The Cobbler was not alone in appreciating the value of clandestine recordings as far as the goings-on at Gala Theatre are concerned, but there will be more about that later.

The mystery deepened when a letter came from Inspector Jamie McAlloon saying that the Crown Prosecution Service had investigated the Peter Benyon affair and were not taking any action. Furthermore they were not prepared to enter into any more correspondence and that was the end of the enquiry. The Cobbler took it to a solicitor who wrote and asked for the whole thing to be reviewed and sent back to the Crown Prosecution Service. Within a short time **a letter came from Arthur Proud, <u>Head of Police Professional Standards,</u> saying that the matter had been reviewed twice by the Crown Prosecution Service and that was an end of it.** The Cobbler then arranged a meeting with Jeff Corrigan of the Crown Prosecution Service. When he asked Mr Corrigan about the progress of his case, to his surprise **Mr Corrigan told him that the Crown Prosecution Service had never received it.**

Allo, allo, allo, what's going on ere. then? A senior copper says that the CPS has looked at it twice and there's no case to answer. The Head of the Crown Prosecution Service says that the CPS has never seen it. Not even a snifter. Seems a bit suspicious to me, don't you think?

The obscene telephone calls continued, with the police apparently unable to trace the source. The messages, which the Cobbler had taped, had been left on his mobile phone answering service and were a mixture of death threats and abuse. The phone was handed to the police who taped the threats from the phone and returned it. Three weeks later the Cobbler contacted the police, who stated that they were waiting for One2One to respond to them. In frustration the Cobbler contacted One2One himself and was told that no request had been received from Durham Police. Mystified by this response the Cobbler asked the Police for clarification. The Police's response was "Sorry, son, the fax mustn't have gone through."

The excuse the police made was that the number could not be traced because the phone was switched off. After almost a year, and only after contacting OFTEL, his phone service provider (One2one) eventually admitted that the number would be on their database under these circumstances, but it could only be revealed to the police. **The police continued to deny that it was possible to obtain the number of the caller, in spite of being shown the letter from One2one.**

By this time the Cobbler was so concerned about the whole affair that he consulted a solicitor, David Gray & Sons, and was interviewed by a lady called Lisa Jackson.

The way forward, apparently, was to seek a Judicial Review of the circumstances. This was going to be expensive, so legal aid would be needed. Dozens of letters later a statement was prepared, but when the Cobbler was finally allowed to read it he was very dissatisfied because important facts relating to his case had been omitted, omissions that the Cobbler believed would weaken his case considerably. He complained about it to his solicitor and the dispute became more and more heated. The thunderbolt came when David Gray & Sons dropped the Cobbler's case two weeks before the legal deadline for the Judicial Review to go ahead, leaving insufficient time for another firm to take the case over. End of Judicial Review.

The next step is to complain to your solicitor, of course. Then followed a meeting with a wonderful lady called Claire Routledge, the partner of David Gray & Sons who deals with complaints against the firm. This lady appeared to become haughtier and haughtier as the meeting proceeded, until she came out with the statement **"Well I'm a Labour activist."** Ok then, Ms Routledge. **This proves that you're just the right person to be able to deal objectively with a claim against the Labour Party, aren't you?**

The current state of play, as of early 2004, is that the whole matter has been referred to the Office of Supervision of Solicitors, who have referred it to a negligence panel. Four solicitors have declined to represent Tony, and he is still without representation at this time.

The next step he took was a complaint to the Standards Board of England, run by the Office of the Deputy Prime Minister. The motto of this organisation is "Confidence in Local Democracy" which, since it is run by John Prescott, is almost a contradiction in terms. The Cobbler complained that he had been swindled out of election by a councillor and the police refuse to investigate. Coincidentally this Councillor was a member of the Police Complaints Authority. A few weeks later the Cobbler received a standard letter from the Standards Board saying that they had looked into the allegations and could find no basis for them. Since this was a only a preliminary hearing to see if there was any validity in the complaint, no details of the allegations would be posted on the Standards Board website. No, there was no appeals process, Mr Prescott was the final arbiter. You could take the matter to a Judicial Review, of course, but that would be expensive and you would not get legal aid for it.

Overall, a pattern emerges. It seems that there are certain individuals who are, to all intents and purposes, complaint-proof. They do something which is obviously wrong, but when the victim complains you find that all manner of people including

102

police, solicitors, council officers, trade union officials, and MPs seem to be falling over themselves to make sure that this complaint does not get investigated. The worrying thing is that this is by no means an isolated case. Many of the people who go into the Cobbler's shop have exactly the same story to tell. Obvious injustice, which they can only redress with an expensive law suite at their own expense through a legal system in which they have good cause to have little faith.

I have studied a lot of these stories and several familiar patterns seem to emerge. It may be that you are being subjected to a conspiracy of this sort or you may know somebody who is. Look at **Anatomy of a Stitchup** at the end of this book to see if any of this rings true with you. Even if they are not a conspiracy theorist anybody with even the most cursory knowledge of cases like this rapidly comes to the conclusion that whatever the rights and wrongs of any individual case, it seems that there is no quick, accessible system - whether legal or administrative - that provides a transparent and accessible means of redress for the man in the street, or indeed the Cobbler's shop. This is not just my opinion, many lawyers have said it themselves.

Here is one last scary little incident. In early 2003 Tony the Cobbler made it known that he was going to stand as an independent candidate in the local elections, took all of the material out of his window and replaced it with a big poster saying " The Cobbler's election campaign starts soon" Within a couple of weeks a uniformed constable made an excuse to come into the Cobbler's shop for a moment. Just as he was about to leave he turned and said **"Are you standing in these elections?"**

"Yes" was the reply from the Cobbler.

"Well, if you know what's good for you, you won't" said the constable, and jumped into a police car that sped off before the Cobbler could get its number. In conversation with senior policemen about this the Cobbler revealed that he had been given internal police documentation relating to serious police corruption. "If you publish that in your window then it will be a whole new ballgame" commented the officer in charge. From the tone of his voice it was apparent that the ballgame was not going to be tennis, or anything else that the Cobbler might enjoy.

If you had seen the sort of allegations that have been brought into the Cobbler's shop you would understand why the Cobbler took these threats seriously and decided not to stand, knowing as he did that if the police decided to take the threatened action against him he would be completely alone against them, as so many others are. **A common complaint about Durham Police brought into the Cobbler's shop is that you complain about the actions of a policeman, and the**

force refuses to log it.

This is an amazing allegation that is difficult to check under the circumstances. What you can check is the number of allegations made against Durham Police in the national statistics published on the internet. I did so and found that Durham Police had the second lowest number of complaints logged against them, second only to City of London. In fact, **the number of complaints, which Durham Police say they have received, is less than half the national average for all forces in Britain.**

It makes you wonder whether everything is on the straight and level, as the expression goes.

This appears to be the pattern of all the complaints brought into the Cobbler's shop. People with obvious injustices, but everywhere they go their progress is barred by a wall of non-compliance and secrecy. Of course, no chapter on the law would be complete without a reference to lawyers, because each and every little silver slug-like trail seems to end up on the desk of a lawyer somewhere. The lasting legacy of the Blair government is likely to be the way that the law is being used, not to give people justice but to deny them it. It seems that the solicitors are the final guardians of the corrupt councillors and council officers, and past them you will not go.

All roads seem to lead to a Judicial Review, with a solicitor's time costing about £120 per hour. Not much hope for anybody earning minimum wage of around £5 an hour, because you need to work 30 hours of your time to buy one hour of a solicitor's time and believe me, solicitors don't do much in one hour! The Blair government has "ended the gravy-train of legal aid" (Tony's own words) which means that you either put up with injustice or risk tens of thousands of pounds of your own money to take a case to court. One way of stopping "spiralling legal aid costs" ((Blair's own words) would be to put a cap on lawyer's fees. That, of course, would reduce the amount that his wife Cherie and other legal hangers-on would earn, so that's a non-starter. The only other way is to reduce the number of cases going to court under legal aid.

There was a massive surge in criminal negligence cases against the National Health Service. How do you deal with that? Stop legal aid for cases against the NHS, of course. The other way of reducing the legal aid budget was the introduction of the no-win-no-fee system they have in the USA, which led to the ambulance chasing system we have at the moment, where on every street corner you've got somebody asking whether you've had an accident in the past three years that our legal vultures can settle upon. All this amounts to a backdoor privatisation of the legal system, and when was the last time that a privatisation benefited the ordinary man and woman in the street? The biggest of the ambulance chasers, Claims Direct, cherry-picked all the best cases, won a lot of money which they did not pass on to their clients and then went bankrupt. Yes, you can try to sue them; no, you won't get legal aid for it. Once again the little silver trail ends up on a lawyer's desk.

So let's give a big hand to the lawyers, those ultimate guardians of Durham's Councils.

Let's hear it for:

Andrew North   The answer to the eternal question of "who will guard the guardians?" is "Andrew North, Director of Corporate & Legal Services for Durham County Council" Like a lot of people in his position he has a dual role which at times can put him in an difficult position. First and foremost he is the legal representative of the elected members of the Council and the paid officers. Secondly he is the Standards Officer of the Council, responsible for policing the Council. If he finds corruption or malpractice in the Council he is in the awkward position of having to prosecute people he is also paid to protect, a conflict of interest that appears to be intentional. Mr North is in overall charge of all legal dealings within Durham County Council, and therefore is the line-manager for **Leslie Davies**, the solicitor for Durham Police Authority. Once you have finished banging your head against the brick wall of the other police complaints organisations, you will end up talking to Mr North.

A number of County Council employees and ex-employees have had dealings with Mr North in the past and were so dissatisfied with the outcome that they ended up in the Cobbler's Shop. Chief Executive of the County Council, Kingsley Smith, wrote to the Cobbler, indicating that an independent law firm would be contacting him, in accordance with Council regulations, to investigate his complaint. Three weeks went by and a letter came from a Durham County Council officer, Mr Fenwick, telling him that the "independent" law firm, Dickinson Dees, had finished the investigation and ruled in favour of the Council. This came as a surprise to the Cobbler, who had never been contacted by the solicitors, and therefore they could not have seen any of his evidence!

It is safe to publish the fact that Andrew North has spent (some might even go so far as to say wasted) at least half a million pounds on a legal dispute with his opposite number in Darlington over some obscure bitch-fight about the ownership of various bits and pieces around the county, and the loser (actually the loser's taxpayers) will also have to pick up the bill for interest payments of a million pounds. What seems important to me is that half a million pounds that could otherwise have been spent on the old people's homes that Durham County Council are closing because of lack of money has gone to highly paid lawyers instead. Why could John Prescott's office not have stepped in earlier and provided some sort of arbitration to save all this money?

The Cobbler has a lot of documentation relating to the cases of council staff who have spent a great deal of time and money in dispute with Andrew North, but were eventually defeated because of the immense amount of money that he can bring to bear against them, but if you want to watch this man's face change colour dramatically, I witnessed this when the Cobbler quizzed him, barrister style, about the County Council and the Durham County Cricket Club scandal.

Before we leave the subject of Andrew North and his boss Kingsley Smith, it is interesting to note that a little bit of very important history may have been written in their offices. Tony Blair's election agent John Burton has just written an autobiography, and in it he tells us that the legendary meeting at which Gordon Brown stood down in favour of his more photogenic junior Tony Blair in the Labour leadership election stakes, took place not in a posh restaurant in London as we have been allowed to believe, but actually in Kingsley Smith's office in Durham County Hall. Now Gordon wants Tony to follow through with his part of the bargain and stand down during the second term, but Tony seems reluctant to do so. Why don't you go down to the Cobbler's shop and complain about it, Gordon? A lot of other Labour Party people have after dodgy deals cooked up at County Hall.

Lesley Blackie is Andrew North's equivalent on the City Council, and there are similar reservations about her dual role as protector and prosecutor of wrongdoing. For instance she is the one who has refused several members of the public access to information relating to Councillors' expenses, despite allegations by senior Labour Party members that blatant fraud had taken place. There was an infamous City of Durham Constituency Labour Party meeting when it was alleged that one particular Councillor had been caught claiming expenses for being at two meetings that were on at the same time, and had been doing so for years. Honest Labour Councillors were incensed by the fact that he had been caught but was being allowed to pay back the money, amounting to several thousand pounds, over a period of time. The crime was reported to Mr Gibson of Durham Constabulary who, as is usual under such circumstances, refused to investigate it and as a consequence a complaint has been logged against him with the PCA.

When the LibDems took over power this became the responsibility of Sue Pitts. She concluded that the Councillor had only done it a few times, and she did not intend to take any action. So much for LibDem openness and honesty! Lesley Blackie's signature is on the documentation relating to the sale of City Council property at well below market value, and she was also named as a party in a conspiracy to defraud the taxpayer in evidence handed over to the Metropolitan Police on 23rd October 2003

David Gray & Sons who are now facing a negligence panel.

Jeff Corrigan of Durham's Crown Prosecution Service, rumoured to be preparing to take early retirement after the Cobbler attempted to force an investigation into his activities via Kevin Foster Head of Crown Prosecution Service Complaints Section. They are now filing Mr Martin's letters without response.

Close to the top of the legal system food chain are those mysterious but very well paid people, the judges. Thankfully I have had no personal contact with these people (as yet, touch wood) and I hope it stays that way. It seems likely that most judges are honest and discharge their duties to the best of their ability, but it does seem that if you get a wrong 'un it is difficult to do anything about it, because they are answerable only to the Lord Chancellor, the guy who got into so much trouble for wallpapering his office with that incredibly costly wallpaper at taxpayers' expense There are people who have taken that final step, risking their life savings and home on their day in a civil court and regret having done so, because the judges overseeing their cases seem to have become the ultimate guardians of the incompetent and corrupt.

Unlike the USA, where claims for damages are heard by a jury, in the UK the virtues of a case like this are heard and decided by a judge sitting alone. These gentlemen, the ultimate product of the old-boys network, are much less likely to find in favour of the little guy (or gal) and in the rare event that they do, the damages they award are always much less than the USA equivalent. Naturally, the Blair government wants fewer trials-by-jury, and more people tried by magistrates. Why? - because magistrates are much more likely to convict than a jury (tough on crime, tough on the causes of crime), but above all the justice they dole out is cheap, cheap, cheap.

Every now and again you get the names of corrupt judges published on the internet, but the website does not seem to last long. During the Cold War period the government poured lots of resources into places like GCHQ, where foreign intelligence (i.e. spy information) was sifted and collated. Nowadays there is not nearly as much need for that, and most of the work of GCHQ and similar organisations is concerned with tracking political dissidents like the Cobbler. Internet traffic is monitored at a place called Menwith Hill, which monitor and crash websites the government does not like. After the September 11th disaster, the Blair government took on immense new powers that enabled them to censor anything they wanted to, without having to give a reason.

We are living in a country where the law appears to be protecting the criminals, and honest people are being denied justice through the law. All over the country there must be thousands, perhaps tens of thousands of people who have suffered obvious injustice, but like Tony the Cobbler they have run into an impenetrable brick wall of official non-cooperation. They spend their lives writing countless letters to people who are paid to investigate injustice of one sort or another and yet they are still denied justice. They have reached that age-old dilemma of what can you do when the law and justice are in opposition? What can you do when the country is being run by the criminals?

Once again it is very difficult to know where to draw the line on this chapter because the story continues to evolve. I have just returned from the Cobbler's shop where he was fuming at the most recent letter he had received from the Crown Prosecution Service. They do not intend to take any further action, for a variety of reasons. The Cobbler's website was not hacked, **the images were dumped onto his website accidentally.** All I can say is that it sounds like the people who run the Crown Prosecution Service do not update websites very frequently. I do however, and I can tell you that it is impossible to dump anything onto another website accidentally. You need to have access to at least two passwords and a certain amount of other information. If it was possible to dump stuff onto other websites accidentally then the internet would be in chaos. The letter ignores the fact that it was not just a matter of an image being dumped onto the website, the whole website was deleted!

It then goes on to repeat the lie that the Cobbler had said he did not want the boys prosecuted. Of course he wants them prosecuted, that is the whole point of the complaint. It then goes on to say that this decision is final as far as the CPS is concerned, but if you choose to do so then you can challenge them in court. Fat chance of that happening, because the Cobbler feels he has not had the best legal service from David Gray & Sons and he is up against an organisation with an almost infinite amount of lawyers and an infinite amount of time.

To clinch the argument the letter warns that the file has been seen by Sir David Calvert-Smith QC, the Director of Public Prosecutions, who apparently agrees with their decision. This is class, Tony, because it looks like you have just been dumped on by the same people who tried to dump on Paul Burrell, butler to Lady Diana. When the Queen warned "there are forces at work in this country about which we know nothing, Paul" these could have been the people she was warning him about. Yes indeed, Tony, you have been dumped on from a very great height indeed but tell me something, does a caviar-and-champagne fuelled turd smell any better than ordinary bullshit? There may have been a time when somebody with a knighthood commanded automatic respect because it meant that the recipient was particularly brave or particularly noble, but now that the New Year's Honours List is festooned with time-serving civil servants who have done little else for their honours than serve a succession of governments without causing uncomfortable waves, the currency of the knighthood is devalued.

Above all though, the frightening thing is that it seems beyond dispute that in certain circumstances elements within the Government, the Police Force, the Crown Prosecution Service and God-only-knows what else can collaborate to deny an ordinary person justice. For me that is much, much scarier than the rise in street crime or knowing that somebody is waiting outside your shop with a baseball bat ready to break your legs.

Update 16th November 2003

Like most honest citizens my involvement with the police is minimal, but I have just had an instructive little brush with the law myself. A few weeks ago I was driving past the Swallow Hotel in Gateshead, watching my speedometer as I normally do, conscious of the fact that there are speed cameras around. To my surprise a speed camera flashed as I passed by it. I looked down at my speedometer which said 28 miles per hour. It must be a mistake, I thought to myself and kept on driving at well below the thirty limit. As I passed by, camera after camera flashed at me, in fact there were so many flashes I thought that Bonfire Night had come early!

Sure enough, a couple of weeks later the all-too-familiar letter dropped through my door saying that I had been caught on camera doing 37 mph in a 30mph zone. There is no need to go to court, just give us £60 and we'll say no more about it. I wrote back to them saying that I believed that this was a mistake, please show me the evidence. Soon after that I received a letter from Northumbria Police saying that if I wanted to see the evidence I would have to go to court and risk a £1000 fine, so just give us £60 and we will say no more about it. Come on Northumbria police, £1000 is 25% of my annual income as a disabled person, as a punishment for exceeding the speed limit by 7mph - surely not?

Then I look back at some of the stories I have been told about the local police forces and start to believe that it is quite likely that they would. I do not have the courage of people like Tony Martin and Gerry Coulter, and faced with the prospect of further involvement with a police force that seems far more threatening than the small-time criminals they seem to spend most of their time chasing, it seems likely that I will give in to a process that bears a strong resemblance to the crime of demanding money with menaces and simply give them the money they are asking for. There is very little doubt in my mind that Northumbria Police force had their photographic fund-earners turned up a little bit too high that particular night, but realistically there is nothing that I, as an ordinary person, can do to challenge it, as many motorists know to their cost.

Faced with mounting crime that threatens their re-election prospects New Labour are devolving more and more power to the lower end of the criminal justice system, the bobby on the beat and the magistrates court, as a cheap way of doling out makeshift justice. Fixed penalties for a variety of motoring offences proved such a good money spinner they were soon joined by Tony Blair's scheme for fixed penalty tickets for loutish behaviour, a scheme that was initially withdrawn because it was greeted with a hail of press ridicule, then quietly reintroduced when all the fuss died down. Now the ordinary copper has the power to issue on-the-spot fines for all sorts of things, including truancy. Combine this with the abolition of the right to a trial by jury for a whole range of imprisonable offences which are now to be dealt with in a magistrate's court and, you have a cut-price justice system gone crazy, the biggest prison population in Europe and a police force that is way down on a level with politicians in terms of public esteem. It is not a matter of "who will guard the guardians" more a matter of "who will guard us from the guardians

Those of you with internet connections might be interested in the work of a gentleman called Gerry Coulter, whose story of his clash with Dorset Police sounds worthy of a book all to itself. In the meantime, read some of it on www.dorsetpolice.com. _ The story of how he spent £100,000 challenging Dorset Police over the right to use that domain name is fascinating. Some interesting details of the inner workings of Dorset Police and other similar forces can be found at www.dorsetvictimsupport.org and I would suggest that you look at this as soon as possible. He publishes things on this site that nobody else would dare to do, but perhaps the fact that he is a wealthy Japanese-trained martial arts expert has something to do with it.

In the meantime here are a couple of questions you might want to ask your local Chief Constable and MP:

> Durham Constabulary have the second lowest level of complaints logged against their officers in the last published league tables, about half of the national average, and there is overwhelming evidence that Durham Constabulary routinely refuse to log complaints against their own officers. Is it possible that these two facts are related?

> Why do people like Tony Martin find it so very difficult to have their complaints investigated, and why are the most powerful people in the legal system including the Director of Public Prosecutions himself, accepting evidence that is obviously false?

Update 18th November 2003

We are all waiting for the visit to Blair's Sedgefield constituency by George W. Bush. We are told that during his state visit to England he will be surrounded at all times by 700 security men, a tricky operation if he ever needs to visit one of our small English public conveniences, one would have thought. These security people wanted the London Tube system to be closed down and all aircraft flying over London grounded to make sure that the most powerful democratically elected leader in the world is safe from the people. The only contact it seems he will have with the people of this green and unpleasant land will be the Blair family, the other Royal family and a few handpicked Blair constituents at Sedgefield.

He might just catch sight of an overwhelming force of Metropolitan and Durham Police whose leave has been cancelled throughout the week to ensure that no anti-war demonstrators get within banner-waving distance of George Dubyah. The cash to pay their overtime is to come from the same pot of money that my £60 speeding fine has just gone into. 100,000 fixed penalty speeding fines will pay for the Metropolitan Police operation, but Durham Police only need to prosecute 17,000 unwary motorists to pay for Tony and George's brief one million pound fish & chip pub lunch at the Dun Cow Inn, Sedgefield. Value for money?

Chapter 9
Death on the Tyne

Death be not proud, though some have said that thou art Mighty and dreadful, for thou art not so.

John Donne

If you want read something that is spiritually uplifting then skip this chapter because there is nothing in it for you. You might like to try some of the poems of John Donne because his words can convince you of the nobility of death. There is nothing noble about the deaths that are the central part of this story, but for me this chapter is the story that really needs telling. This is the story of the horrific real-life murder of a young mother and her young son, and ever since I received the documentation from Tony the Cobbler I have been unable to stop thinking about it. The story reads like fiction but every single word is fact.

I like to start each chapter with a little bit of a laugh, some light entertainment before getting down to the real business of taking the piss out of politicians. This one has got to be different though, because even after days of turning the facts over in my mind I cannot think of one single funny thing to say about it. This is a horrific double murder that was avoidable, and happened because Tory politicians wanted to save money and Labour politicians wanted to win an election and denigrate the Cobbler. To me each chapter of this book has a colour and the colour of this one is dirty grey, the colour of the dust that comes off onto your fingers when you rub them along the metalwork of the docks at North Tyneside, where this took place.

As I have said before, there are episodes in the story of Tony Martin that would be hard to believe if the documentation to prove them were not available to me. I have that documentation here beside me as I peck at the keyboard of my computer with my untrained right forefinger, trying to get the story down on paper. Amongst it there is an article cut from Private Eye of March 2001 entitled "Death on the Tyne," a duck egg-green covered folder headed "Newcastle & North Tyneside Health Authority Inquiry re Raymond Wills" the killer at the centre of this story, and a Northern Echo article written by Mark Summers dated 27th February 2001 headlined "Killer should have been put in hospital months before tragedy" which has a picture of the Cobbler standing outside of his shop.

Without this evidence even I would probably have dismissed the Cobbler's claims of involvement in this tragedy as pure fantasy, because when you start talking about the needless murder of a mother and son by an untreated chronic schizophrenic the brain recoils from the horror of it all, and the imagination tries to re-classify it into the grey half-world of fictional violence as a defence. Thankfully that is where the vast majority of us will meet the sort of event I am describing here, and over and over again I have to keep telling myself this is real, this really happened. This story has come to haunt me as I look at the cold resentful eyes of Raymond Wills and the first (and last) infant school photograph of his five year-old nephew Ashley Wills, one of his victims. It is as if they want their story to be told, and I am the one they have chosen to tell it. Here it is.

I suppose you could say that this incident is a legacy of the Thatcher era. The disadvantage of a book that is so critical of the Labour Party is that it gives you a reason to forget just how bad things were under the Tories. Margaret Thatcher, the grandmother of all hard-nosed politicians, looked at the North-East of England and made a mental note of the fact that most of it had been staunch Labour for as long as there had been a Labour to be staunch about. Why try to persuade these people to vote for me? It's a waste of time. Let's use this area as an example of what happens if you get on the wrong side of Margaret Almighty. That is how the miners' strike and the death of the British coalmining industry happened, remember?

Bit by bit resources were pulled out of the North and used to make life easier for the true-blue South of England. Life is all about winners and losers, and the homeland of the natural born winner is the square mile of London's financial centre. If you lived within commuting distance of that you deserved to be taken seriously and everywhere else in the country fell under the general heading of "Elsewhere." Resources were withdrawn stealthily from public sector areas like health and education because the winners did not use them as long as there were good private schools and BUPA around. The main thrust of Thatcher's public sector reforms was they should become efficient, spelt C-H-E-A-P A-S P-O-S-S-I-B-L-E.

We will almost certainly never get to know the name of the person responsible for the wonderful bit of NHS cost-cutting that came to be known as "Care in the Community." The logic of the exercise probably went like this. Rich people vote for us, so we need to keep them happy by taking less from them in tax. No problem, we can do that, and the next minute Nigel Lawson cut the top rate of Income Tax from 60% to 40%, with the Daily Mail trumpeting the headlines "Spend, Spend, Spend!" Step two is to save money on the things we do for the non-Tory voting poor. The biggest expense is the NHS, so why not close a few hospitals?

There were tens of thousands of long-term patients of one sort or another, many with mental illnesses, taking up expensive bed space. Why not move them out of hospitals into cheaper accommodation somewhere, and put Social Services in charge of them? One look at the predicted costing of the exercise, with a tasteful red border around it saying "Cheap, Cheap, Cheap...." convinced the Cabinet waverers at a stroke. Yes, the downside is that we would be releasing a lot of mentally ill people into the community, but if anything goes wrong we can always blame those lazy, longhaired socialist social workers. After all, these poor people would benefit from contact with society. If anybody in the Tory Party ever asked whether Margaret thought that society would benefit from direct contact with tens of thousands of mentally ill people roaming the streets, they were probably reminded that Thatcher Almighty didn't believe that society existed and the plan went ahead.

The focus of our story now moves to the wrong side of the North-South divide, to the terraced house in North Tyneside where Tony Martin lives with his wife and two children. I want you to try to imagine that you are this man trying to keep your business as a cobbler going single-handedly, because your father has had a nervous breakdown, as well as battling against corruption in local government and the police force. You then spend an hour or so getting through the traffic, trying to get through the Tyne Tunnel to get home to North Shields. What would you want when you got there? Peace and quiet, I would imagine. What would be the last thing you would want? How about being woken up in the middle of the night by the screams of a chronic schizophrenic that the Council had moved into the house next door?.

It took quite a lot of effort before the Cobbler finally got Warren Austin and Ralph Blundell of North Tyneside Council to admit that the house next door to his had been bought up and used as a hostel for mentally ill Care-in-the-Community refugees by a privatised organisation known as Enterprise 5. By this time his wife and two children, tired of having their night's sleep disturbed by the constant commotion next door, were living with Tony's mother-in-law. They say that bad things happen in threes, and if the appearance of Tony's new neighbours was bad thing number one and family moving out number two, then the re-appearance of an old acquaintance called Stevo in the Cobbler's life was definitely disaster number three

Let me take a few moments to tell you about Stevo. Stevo is not actually his real name, but I am sure you can recognise the type. He is the sort of person who, when he appears in a pub everybody looks away and says "Oh God, there's Stevo" hoping he won't notice them. Of course, Stevo does notice and comes to sit beside you.

Stevo is the one who will just not take the hint and stay away. He is the one who gets into fights with people for no good reason, gets the sh*t kicked out of him and comes back for more the next day. The word "embarrassment" was thought up especially for the Stevos of this world

Everybody has a Stevo in his or her life, but this is Super-Stevo. Whether by nature, nurture, the high lead level in the pipes at North Tyneside or his mother dropping a lot of acid in the Sixties, this Stevo is one of a special breed, with all sense of relationship to fellow humans somehow absent. If you think that you have been unfortunate enough to meet one of these people, walk (but don't run) as quickly as you can in the opposite direction.

One minute The Cobbler was sitting at home alone in his house, along comes Stevo and the next minute a party was going on. Well, it was not exactly a party, more like a whole lot of people who you don't really like sitting around in your house drinking and making a lot of noise - the sort of thing that tends to happen when you have a Stevo around. Just as the party was reaching the height of its drudgery, Tony's Care-in-the-Community neighbour chose to start his nightly wailing at the moon.

"That c*nt's not spoiling my f*cking party" shouted Stevo, jumping up from the armchair where he had been sprawled. Next moment he was outside, hammering away at the door of the neighbour's house with his fists. "Come out, you c*nt, I'm going to f*cking kill ya" was the invitation. If his aim was to quieten the Cobbler's neighbour down, the plan needed a rethink, because the screaming went up an octave and took on a banshee-like overtone. Driven to greater heights of desperation by this, Stevo started to kick at the door. The resounding thuds echoed down the street and one by one lights began to come on in the neighbouring houses.

Suddenly he leapt backwards like a startled alley-cat as a gigantic hunting knife poked out of the letter-box, missing his genitals by a fraction of an inch. Stevo seemed frozen to the spot as the blade of the knife rotated, stabbing backwards and forwards as if looking for something.

"F*cking hell, did you see that? The c*nt tried to cut my f*cking d*ck off with that f*cking great knife! He's a f*cking nutter - he needs f*cking locking up!" If you know a Super-Stevo then you will already know that they have a talent, often their only talent, for stating the obvious, and this one was no exception. "I'm f*cking getting out of here. Tony, I don't know how you can f*cking live next door to that c*nt. If it was me I would get the coppers onto him, son." If it had been anybody else, the Cobbler might have explained that he had tried to get the police, social services, North Tyneside Health Authority and just about everybody else involved in the situation. However Stevo had already disappeared around the corner, and was no doubt already relating the story of his brush with danger to some luckless passer-by.

If any of this description sounded comical then I have given you the wrong impression because the whole incident had a scary surrealism that is impossible to convey in words. In a movie this might have seemed funny, but in real life it was one of these split seconds of slow-moving horror that seemed to last for an eternity. As I have said before there are episodes in The Cobbler's story where comedy and tragedy seem to be only a hair's width apart, and if you do not know what that means then you should be grateful that you have never had to experience it.

Within a very short time things started to take a distinct turn for the worse. Tony's neighbour tried to drag a thirteen year-old girl into a back lane. They got as far as the entrance before the girl's screams were answered by seventeen-year-old Alan Burgo, who rescued her. Before long a vigilante-style gang of mid-teenagers were stoning the house next door and the Cobbler, fearful of his own windows, went out to try to calm them down. They were really little more than children, and a few hard words saw them on their way. Not so the men who arrived the next day. These guys were big and angry, not looking to be put off from doing serious injury to the abductor and anybody else who got in their way.

"F*ck off, this is none of your business." Was the greeting the Cobbler received when he went out to find out what the disturbance in the street was all about. "He's a f*cking paedophile, he tried to rape my sister and I'm going to cut his f*cking balls off. So f*ck off back into your house there and mind your own business" From the expression on his face he was not exaggerating his intention, the Cobbler thought to himself. He tried to cool the situation down but one of them saw Wills walking up the road to his house and the gang took off down the street hurling abuse at him.

It took a while for the Cobbler to persuade the authorities that there was a very real problem. He showed them the many letters he had written to a wide variety of agencies asking for help and warning that the young man in the house next door was seriously mentally ill. Now even the police were ready to believe him. Eventually they persuaded the young man to open his door, and they went in. Not long after this Wills was moved away and that was the last time the Cobbler saw him. Tony believes that if he had not been moved there was a very real possibility that the tragedy that followed could have happened to his own family.

The rest of the story has been pieced together from a number of sources, but most of it lies here on my desk written in the dry clinical style of the report of the Newcastle & North Tyneside Health Authority Inquiry, and you have to read between the lines to comprehend the full horror of what happened next. Once again I have to remind myself that this is a real-life tragedy unfolding here.

The Cobbler notified North Tyneside Council, Social Services and Enterprise 5 about the incident, but by now he was well known to Chris Lennie of the Northern Region Labour Party and the dirty-tricks and spin machinery was switched to top gear at Labour North headquarters. Rather than doing something constructive which could have averted the tragedy, Lennie and Rita Stringfellow, Leader of Labour-controlled North Tyneside Council, seem to have concentrated their efforts on attempting to rubbish the Cobbler's reputation by spreading a rumour that his election campaign was funded by the Tories. One of the Cobbler's newspaper contacts phoned him up one afternoon telling him that he had just finished talking to Chris Lennie, and that Lennie had asked that his newspaper run a story saying so, and that he had refused.

Meanwhile Raymond Wills was moved to another Care-in-the-Community house in Sallyport Crescent in Newcastle, but the Cobbler's warning of the man's violent behaviour went unheeded and his level of supervision was not increased. Perhaps it was thought that if too much was made of the incident it might get into the papers and enhance the Cobbler's reputation. That was the last thing that Chris Lennie and the rest of the Labour Party wanted.

It was several months before the Cobbler found out what had happened. The police were alerted by Ken Wills, the father of Raymond, after a phone call from his son. He was very upset, and all he would say is "Dad , I've killed Caroline and the bairn." The police went to the house in Cramlington where 26 year-old Caroline Wills and her five year-old son Ashley were staying, and as they opened the unlocked door a horrific scene met their eyes. In the middle of the small living room were the bodies of a young woman and a small boy, both obviously dead. Standing beside them was Craig Pattison, Caroline Wills fiancé, who was first to arrive on the scene, rigid with shock.

A subsequent autopsy showed that almost one hundred stab-wounds from a large hunting knife had been inflicted on the two bodies, with repeated frenzied blows to the neck and throat of the young boy almost severing the head from the shoulders.

Raymond Wills himself was found upstairs in his own home sobbing, with the bloodstained knife beside him. It was quite some time before he was able to tell his story. When he did so it was told in a detached, almost third person style, as if he was merely an observer of the tragedy. Raymond had had mental problems since his teens, and had been diagnosed as a paranoid schizophrenic. He had planned the murder well in advance, with the large hunting knife bought specially for the purpose from a stall in the Granger Market at Newcastle. He had sat looking at it for weeks, trying to pluck up enough courage to use it, and it was probably the same knife he had brandished through the letterbox at Stevo that night in North Tyneside.

Over and over again he had asked for help, even threatening to commit suicide. Many people had warned the authorities about his problems but the lack of resources for mentally ill patients was so acute that only those who were a proven danger to other people could be accommodated as in-patients. He loved his sister and nephew, but seemed to be resentful of the attention they were getting from his parents. The plan was to kill his sister and nephew and then himself so that they could somehow be together and be happy forever, because he did not want to be alone.

In desperation he had gone to his sister's home and eventually persuaded her to open the door. Then he barged through and stabbed her repeatedly in the chest and stomach before cutting her throat. Her screams woke five year-old Ashley who ran downstairs to find out what was going on. Wills let go of his sister, grabbed Ashley and started to stab him. When he was sure they were both dead he telephoned his father, told him what he had done, went home and went upstairs with the intention of killing himself. The police arrived before he had the time and courage to do so.

Put into these words it sounds almost trivial, but please remember for a moment that we are talking about a real-life occurrernce.. The man wielding the knife was somebody who desperately needed help, and asked for it, but he was denied it to save money so that politicians could make further tax cuts to enhance their chances of re-election.

The Cobbler tried to lodge complaints about Rita Stringfellow for leaking confidential information about his collaboration with Tory candidate Nick Cartmell to the press, but all complaints about Labour politicians went to the desk of Chris Lennie at the new Labour North headquarters in North Tyneside, and no further. David Chambers, Head of the Complaints Department at Labour-controlled North Tyneside Council simply responded by saying that it was not possible to lodge a complaint against the leader of a council, and the only possible route of complaint was the Local Government Ombudsman. Ombudsmen in England can investigate and make recommendations, but apart from that they are essentially toothless. Even as late as February 2004 Council Officers such as Mr D Patterson, Manager of Finance & Administration at North Tyneside Council were still intent on shifting the blame around, and once again we have the smell of an unsavoury cover-up.

This was confirmed by Jeff Kay of North Tyneside Council in one of their Council's classic "evasions, half-truths & downright lies" letters.

Meanwhile, all was not well within the ranks of North Tyneside local Labour Party. There was to be an election to decide who was going to be the local mayor and the grass-roots activists were unhappy about what was going on in the party at local level. This eventually crystallised into a report called "Serving our Community" that was sent to the NEC, the Labour Party's National Council. All you need to do is read the headings to understand the internal dissent. "Lack of Democratic Discussion" "Expulsions" "Violence against Labour Councillors" "Victimisation of Council Officers" "Undermining the Position of Dr David Clark MP" "Predjudice in Resource Allocation" "Register of Outside Interests" "The Abolition of the Equal Rights Subcommittee" and "The Numbers Game."

The split in the local Labour Party ranks grew wider and the grass-roots activists lost interest, culminating in the election of a Tory mayor. John Marsdon was drafted to a leading role in a hope that he could lead the Council out of its multi-million pound financial defecit, which at one point was so bad that the Council was unable to set a budget. In late 2003 Rita Stringfellow and seven other Councillors announced they were standing down, for reasons that remain unexplained, but it is known that police had been drafted in after allegations concerning North Shields Fish Quay Festival and concerns over the activities of the Social Services Department.

Of course, nothing happened as a consequence of the submission of the local Labour Party's report to the NEC because, under the leadership of Tony Blair, the whistle-blowers within the Labour Party are treated as the worst criminals of all, and dissent is the greatest crime of all because blind obedience has become the New Labour watchword. Not to be outdone the Cobbler made 500 copies of the report and distributed them around North Tyneside, as well as thousands of leaflets with the motto "A vote for Labour in North Tyneside is a vote for corruption." Whether or not his efforts altered the outcome of the election we will never really know, all we do know is that Labour lost and North Tyneside. The fact that this mayor eventually had to resign after allegations of child sex abuse is another matter, of course.

The story of the tragedy of the Wills family continues to haunt me. The pages of these reports are simply the tip of an iceberg of suffering for them and those like them. I feel continuously drawn to the portrait of young Ashley Wills in his first and last school photograph, not knowing whether or not to smile as you do when you are only five years old and facing the uncertainties of the school photographer for the first time. I have worked with children most of my adult life and hate to see them hurt, because there is more than enough time for pain and suffering when you are grown up. Perhaps it is his spirit that is with me as I write this.

I am sorry about the bitterness in this chapter. The essence of this story is that two people were murdered needlessly as a consequence of a cost-cutting exercise in the NHS to fund Tory tax cuts, but Rita Stringfellow of North Tyneside Council and Chris Lennie do not emerge entirely blameless. In 1997 we were all tired of Tory corruption and voted in Labour to do something about it and close the inequality gap between the rights of the rich and poor. We were betrayed, because the gap between the rich and poor has broadened under Blair and he is using the law to deny ordinary people their rights. Now we are seeing the true colours of New Labour with the Hutton enquiry into the death of David Kelly, and it seems to me that all of the revelations of New Labour cynicism revealed there were foreshadowed by the way that Chris Lennie treated the problems in Durham and North Tyneside in a way that minimised the daamage to the reputation of Labour North.

This story is all about the blood of two innocent people being spilt needlessly. The real tragedy is that we can visualise the blood of two people, but the spilling of the blood of thousands is beyond our comprehension. It can be nothing more than a statistic to us even when we see it every day in Iraq on the evening news. New Labour has used its power of spin to cover up so much corruption and injustice while a whole generation of young people in the North-East are sinking into apathy and drug-abuse because there is no meaningful work for them to do as the manufacturing sector, for so long the life-blood of Durham's economy, is whittled away. That is not what I and the thousands of others who voted Labour wanted or expected, and the likelihood is that we will never again bring ourselves to trust Labour sufficiently to vote for them again.

We are told that you are concerned about your place in history Tony. Your place in history may be as the man who finally did what Thatcher tried to do but failed - destroy the Labour Party. In the meantime you have got work to do. You have just expelled George Galloway MP for bringing the Labour Party into disrepute over things he said about the war in Iraq. This investigation was organised by Chris Lennie. In this chapter we have shown that Chris Lennie and Rita Stringfellow could have done much more to avoid circumstances that led up to a horrific double murder. George Galloway was expelled from the Labour Party for bringing it into disrepute for doing nothing more than speaking his mind, however wrong you believe his opinion to be. Unless the Labour Party is to be branded hypocritical forever the allegations against Stringfellow and Lennie must be investigated.

Gerry Steinberg MP must join them because there is mounting evidence that he too is in the habit of ignoring evidence of massive corruption in Durham City, and the only person to whom you can complain about if you get no satisfaction from Steinberg is Chris Lennie, who simply refuses to reply to any complaints. If this does not bring the Labour Party into disrepute then nothing does. What happened to the Newcastle & North Tyneside Health Authority Inquiry re Raymond Wills and the Cobbler's evidence in the green-green covered folder? For several months the Cobbler telephoned North Tyneside cCouncil asking about it, and was told that it was *sub judice,* so nothing could be done. He waited a few more months and telephoned again, only to be told that the enquiry had closed and nobody within the Council had been found to be at fault. No, the enquiry could not be re-opened, the deadline had passed.

Perhaps Harry Potter should take time away from Hogwarts School to study North Tyneside's state-of-the-art smoke and mirrors, now-you-see-it, now-you-don't style of trickery. It would be nice to think of the spirit of young Ashley Wills holding the hand of his mother Caroline as they queue outside of a cinema waiting to see "The Prisoner of Azkaban," like so many other families this Christmas 2003. Perhaps all has been forgiven in the hereafter and Uncle Raymond is there with them as well. They deserve some happiness because it is quite plain that they were denied it while alive. That would provide the happy ending this story so desperately needs.

Chapter 10
Election Time

The truth is a heady wine. You should not overestimate people's capacity for it.
Winston Churchill

<u>**Wednesday 12th November 2003**</u>

For one moment the whole of the political world appeared to stand still, because this was the moment they had all been waiting for. It was the first Prime Minister's Question Time with the new Tory leader Michael Howard in control. Anyone with any sort of interest in politics was glued to a television, awaiting this ultimate confrontation of Tory barrister versus Labour barrister. Nor were we disappointed either, because you might not like these people but they certainly can argue and in reality these two men were firing the very first real shots of the next election campaign. Dangerous stuff - don't try this at home, boys and girls!

Rupert Murdoch certainly liked what he saw, because he made one of his rare appearances on his own TV network saying that he was unsure which of these two he and his Sun/Times/Sky TV cohort were going to support at the next election. That must have given Blair and the rest of New Labour something extra-special to put to their focus groups the next day. You had better watch out for Mr Murdoch, Tony, because as your Texan friends might say "You've been kissed but you ain't been loved, boy!"

We all know that opinion manipulation for general elections is done almost entirely through the media of TV and newspapers, but local elections are usually quite different. Try to imagine yourself in Durham City just before the County Council Elections, 21st May 2001. This was showdown time, Tony Martin (Cobbler Anti-Corruption) versus Peter Thompson (Labour.)

Just down from the railway station lies County Hall, operational headquarters of the County Council, and perhaps soon to be the site of the Regional Assembly. Somewhere deep inside this building a plot was thickening. At all costs the Cobbler must be prevented from winning the Gilesgate & Pelaw seat, and a number of talented individuals were brought to bear. It may be a coincidence that Frazer Davies, Press Officer for Durham County Council, had a son who was good with computers, and unlike almost every other teenager in Durham, this young man seems to have suddenly developed an interest in local politics. Even more of a coincidence is the fact that while surfing the net one day, he "inadvertently" happened to dump images of two scantily dressed young girls performing a sex act onto the Cobbler's website, complete with a caption "Cobblers to the Council" on it. Very careless, James!

By a further almost incredible coincidence the presence of this shameful display was leaked to   BBC Look North on February 13th, the day before the Cobbler's Documentary on Close-Up North on the 14th which exposed the infamous cleaning materials scam in Durham City Council (*Remember that one? It went something like this: "Psst.....wanna buy a bottle of special industrial strength Durham City Council bleach?.....Seventeen quid to you.......Yes I know you can buy it for £1.75 in the shops......Yeh, but this lot is special......What's special about it ....I dunno, but Maurice Crathorne uses it all the time....No? Ok suit yourself.....How about property? I can do you a nice sports centre cheap, they've all got to go before the LibDems get in.....*

The next step was to draw the attention of the voting public to the fact that the Cobbler was displaying pornography on his website. A computer at Durham Johnston Comprehensive School, and a lad called Luke Wilson (who by some extraordinary coincidence has a mother who is secretary to Ken Manton, Leader of Durham County Council)   broadcast the news far and wide. This happened just before the election so that the Cobbler did not have time to do anything about it before election day. Mud sticks, particularly if   computer pornography and child molestation allegations are concerned. Most of the voting public don't know enough about computers at that time to know what is going on anyway. All they know was Cobbler + computer porno = bad man. No vote for you, Mr Cobbler!

Councillor Thompson looked up at his framed photograph of himself shaking hands with Tony Blair and he knew everything would be alright. They are really pulling out all of the stops to get me elected, he thought. After all the fuss had died down, if the Cobbler complained, then the usual smoke-and-mirrors trickery would put any complaint into endless delay

Meanwhile up at the Cobbler's shop, the day was becoming a real nightmare. At about ten o' clock one of the Cobbler's regular informants came hurrying into the shop.

"Did you know that they're saying you're a convicted rapist at the polling stations?" she asked. Silly sort of question, really, because anybody who knew the

Cobbler at all would realise that if he knew that the Labour Party were spreading rumours like that he would be out of his shop like a shot, go up to the Labour Party polling headquarters and start tearing people limb from limb. Which is more or less what his intention were as he sped up the street seconds later.

The Cobbler did not expect to be elected as a County Councillor because he knew the power of the election machine he was up against. All of the axes he had to grind were with Durham City Council and that is when he intended to pull out all of the stops. He regarded this election as a practise for the City Council elections in two years time, so he had done almost no canvassing, and the sum total of his election staff, pitted against the might of the Labour election machine. was 76 year-old Ronnie Ormeston and his equally aged bike. Nevertheless a principle is a principle, and if you are going to take the Cobbler's name in vain then you have got to be prepared to face the consequences.

"What would John Major do if this happened to him?" the Cobbler mused to himself as he drove up Gilesgate bank. He had met the ex-Prime Minister a few days before when Nick Cartmell, the Tory candidate in the Parliamentary election going on at the same time, had invited him to a meal at the local Conservative Association. He had no time to think that through any further because by then he was outside the Gilesgate bungalow surrounded by the red rose posters. Looking through the door he could see figures hunched over computers monitors, others arranging pieces of paper. This hive of activity ceased completely as the Cobbler's thunderous hammering on the door threatened to damage the foundations.

"It's the Cobbler, it's the Cobbler!" The inside of the room started to resemble a termite nest that had been kicked open as bewildered Labourites sought the safety of the darker corners of the room.

"Get out here, you b*stards!" Tactful as ever, the Cobbler would not be denied an explanation. Looking through the window there was no movement "Thompson, get out here now!" Bang Bang Bang went the door again, this time neighbours curtains started to twitch uncertainly.

Peter Thompson swallowed hard, did his best to summon up the facial expression he kept for use when he was passing a severe sentence from the magistrate's bench and moved towards the door. He opened it and was confronted by the red faced, angry Cobbler.

"Have you been spreading rumours that I'm a convicted rapist?" By now most of

Gilesgate knew the reason for the Cobbler's visit and interest was mounting in the neighbourhood.

"No, it wasn't me" replied the Justice of the Peace, somewhat taken aback at being spoken to in this manner. "Shit, shit, shit" he thought to himself . " I should have said something like , er, I have no idea what you are talking about." It sounds less suspicious. "I don't know what you are talking about" he stammered.

"Don't give me that bullshit" the Cobbler replied, eyes blazing.

"Go and see for yourself" Thompson replied.

"I will" said the Cobbler, turning towards the polling station.

For a while he watched the large cars with Red Rose banners ferrying the pensioners to the polls. Suddenly a band of young women appeared shouting abuse at him. "Go on, f*ck off, we don't want perverts like you around here!"

"What are you talking about? Hang on, what's going on here?" This was addressed to Peter Thompson who was dropping off another load of potential votes. Quickly, our Justice of the Peace slammed his door shut and sped off, missing the Cobbler by a hair's width as he did so. "All right, if that's the way he wants to play it, that's the way it is" thought the Cobbler, climbing back into his car. Election or no election, people needed their shoes mending.

The count for the all-important parliamentary seat took place that evening, with the County seat returns being counted the following day. Nick Cartmell, the Tory candidate had chosen the Cobbler as one of his observers for the evening parliamentary count, and by 10 pm. the Cobbler had not yet calmed down from his meeting with Peter Thompson. As he walked through the door, his eye lit upon a gentleman (for want of a better word) standing next to Gerry Steinberg MP. This "gentleman" is the person referred to earlier who, it is alleged, has a liking for small boys and camping trips, but for legal reasons we will not be more specific than that.

If you want to simulate the effect of this confrontation upon the Cobbler, I would suggest you find a particularly short tempered, sex-starved Spanish fighting bull that has just come home from a very bad day in the bullring to find that his tea is not ready, and then wave a large red rag in front of it.

"Hello *******, " the Cobbler said. "I am coming after you! You don't know me but I know all about you and what you've been doing to boys!"

Within seconds the room was in uproar. Councillor Joe Knight stepped between the two, attempting to look menacing .

"Would you like to come outside?" Joe asked. All day the Cobbler had been looking for something or somebody to take his anger out on, and this seemed like a heaven-sent opportunity.

"I most certainly would" replied the Cobbler. Nick Cartmell was beginning to regret his choice of observer, and started to count the potential cost of the legal damages on his well-manicured barrister's fingers.

By now the two combatants were outside the door, and Joe Knight was beginning to have doubts about the wisdom of his challenge. His opponent looked younger, fitter and stronger than he was and above all very, very angry. Perhaps diplomatic action rather than mortal combat would be an expedient course of action

"What's your name?" the Cobbler shouted.

"Joe Knight" Mr Knight replied.

"I've got stuff about you in my window" the Cobbler continued. "You and Mick Bennett were the ones who pissed off the Labour Party by nominating that Independent guy, Jeff Lodge, instead of Eileen Rochford for Mayor as a favour for Maurice Crathorne, aren't you?"

By this time Patricia Conway was leading the sobbing (alleged) paedophile out of the room, and passed between Knight and Cobbler. "You are a disgrace" she accused, staring at the Cobbler.

"You are a disgrace for helping that scum" retorted the Cobbler. Joe Knight had mysteriously disappeared and been replaced by two angry looking policemen.

"You're intimidating people" one of them accused.

"I'm just doing your job" the Cobbler replied. "There's a child-molester in there, go in and arrest him." The policeman's face softened.

"Look, between you and me the lads down at the station all think you're doing a grand job with your campaign, but you're going about this all the wrong way. Get back in there and give them hell, but don't intimidate anybody or we'll have to put you out, OK?" Taken aback by meeting a sympathetic copper, the Cobbler agreed and returned   quietly to the counting room. The whole room fell silent as the Cobbler re-entered. Everybody felt sure he would   be enjoying the hospitality of Durham Police station by now. The Cobbler remained, staring at Steinberg and his dubious friend.

The count itself was without further incident. Gerry Steinberg retained his seat, and breathed a sigh of relief. Nick Cartmell, the barrister Tory candidate, also breathed a sigh of relief because he had not been elected, since an MP's salary would have meant a massive pay-cut for him. Joe Knight and Patricia Conway breathed a sigh of relief because it meant that they did not have to be near the Cobbler anymore. The Cobbler breathed a sigh of relief because he did not have to be near the Labour people. The police just breathed a sigh of relief.

Next day's City Council turned out to be a bit of an anti-climax. The Tory candidate, who knew he did not have a cat-in-hell's chance of being elected failed to turn up. Anji Rae, the LibDem candidate who stated that she was only doing it for fun (she is now a LibDem City councillor) appeared to enjoy the proceedings even though she did not get a great deal of votes. The tension mounted as the Labour and Cobbler piles of votes appeared to be going neck-and-neck, with Peter Thompson sweating visibly. Eventually, when the count took place and his victory by 300 votes announced, his face broadened into a smile. A brief token handshake with his opponents and he was gone. His sigh of relief as he left the building could have been heard over at the other side of County Durham.

This defeat only served to strengthen the Cobbler's determination, because his real ambition was to become a City Councillor rather than a County Councillor, and his first taste of a full meeting of Durham City Council left him in no doubt that there was something very wrong going on. The main item on the agenda was to set (in other words increase by a great deal) the Council Tax. If you have never been to one of these meetings then you have missed a great treat, and I can thoroughly recommend it. If you can ignore the fact that the whole process is simply a way of rubber-stamping the corrupt activities of the inner-core City Council cabinet and simply enjoy the pageantry and the ceremony, it is reasonably entertaining.

As an observer you sit in a large room in the Town Hall, staring at the ancient wooden roof decorated with coats of arms and gargoyles. Around you are large portraits of past Gentry who have served their time and no doubt rendered service to the City of Durham. To my mind the smug look on their faces probably suggests that they have been well rewarded in return, but of course cynicism is burnt into my soul after living so long in The Land of the Prince Bishops.

I remember observing one meeting of the full Council that took place well before the 2003 Labour bloodbath. The room hushed as the procession began to enter in their colourful costumes. The Mayor, resplendent in his chain of office provided the focus of attention while behind him looking a little less resplendent, was his deputy and Joe Knight, the Mayor Who Never Was, trailed behind these two, looking not at all resplendent. Next came a lady dressed like a head teacher followed by two elderly bodyguards hobbling along manfully on their walking sticks and behind them came the grey suited officers of the Council, briefcases clasped in red hands. Last of all, perhaps you might say leaving the worst till last, came the dour and flatulent councillors led by the leader of Durham City Council. Maurice Crathorne

They sat down in their groupings according to political affiliation. Labour was in the majority and sat in a large heterogeneous mass in the centre. Facing them, like Custer's last stand, were the six LibDems led by Sue Pitts. Finally, forced to sit in the corner by herself like a naughty schoolgirl was Mildred Brown, still smarting from her (nominal) ejection from the Labour Party for racial abuse of a City Council officer. She sits alone and unsmiling, her thin scarlet painted lips pursed throughout the proceedings.

At the Mayor's right hand side, in a grey pinstriped suit is dumpy little Colin Shearsmith, shining as if he had been freshly oiled for the proceedings. His resemblance to a large silver slug is so overwhelming I look down involuntarily to see whether there is a shiny silver trail where he has been. No, to my disappointment none is visible. I make a mental note to bring a bag of salt next time to test my hypothesis further, and spend the next ten minutes visualising the Chief Executive squirming into a large foamy ball.

I am snapped back to reality as Maurice Crathorne stands up in his capacity as Leader of the City Council and proposer of the motion. A thin foxy gentleman with 50's style teddy-boy sideburns, this man may look like a down-and out country & western vocalist but he has the future of one of Europe's best-known heritage sites in his power. With all the money he's siphoning off, why can't he afford a decent haircut? Concentrate, he's starting to speak.

"I propose to raise the Council Tax by seventeen-and-a half-percent. I know it is a lot, and it is the third year in a row that we have done this, but there is f*ck all you can do about it, because these dummies behind me will back me up, won't you, dummies?"

This is not actually what was said, but that is more or less what he meant. Some of the dummies made positive sounding noises, many did not. One cabinet member seemed to be preoccupied with balancing his enormous bulk on the relatively small chair he had been given, while another had moved without being told to do so and appeared to have got his strings tangled up with the dummy next to him. Together they jerked convulsively, but the rest appeared to have glazed over, awaiting the fullness of time and the promise of free drinks in the bar of the Gala Theatre.

The large gentleman now got to his feet, and I am struck with the resemblance this person has to an illustration of Humpty Dumpty I used to have in a book of nursery rhymes many years ago. I have difficulty concentrating on what he says him as he seconds Maurice's motion.

"Well ah divn't naw aboot ye lads, but ahs ganna dee whorever Morris tells us ta dee, cos 'e might be an ugly lookin' c*nt, but yacun be sartun that comes pay-day e'll see yus all reet with a few quid in ya back pocket if ya dee." Again this is not actually what was said, but it is most certainly what he meant. He paused to look around, perhaps looking for approval from Crathorne and his comrades. Finding none he continues. "Now let's get all this slaver-on owwer win, cos we wastin' good drinken time here and ah's chowkin. Ah god, that LibDem woman Pitts wants ta say summat. Just talk amongst yesells for a bit, lads.". He looks around once more, this time perhaps looking for a wall to sit on to rest his already tiring legs. Unable to find one he points his enormous buttocks in the general direction of the chair he is unable to see, and sits. The chair's protesting squeak echoes around the room, but his aim is true and the docking process is completed successfully. Neighbours on both sides breath a sigh of relief.

Sue Pitts, LibDem leader stands up, shouting over the noise of the meeting . "This is a disgrace. This is the third year in a row that there has been a massive increase. It will not be like this when the LibDems ....."

Foxy Crathorne leaps to his feet. "All reet, we've heard enough of your slaver, missus, coz neebody's liznun ta yah. An as far as yeh lot getten elected's consarned, all ah can say is divven't hold thee breath. We both know ya could put a monkey up for election rund here and if it was a Labour monkey it'd get elected

"Bah, bah," the Labour members rocked backwards and forwards in delight at their leader's rebuttal of the LibDem's arguments.

"See worra mean?" taunts Crathorne. "OK, letsava vote on it. If yeh's all agree with whatever I say whenever ah says it, put yeh's hands up." The hands of the Labour front benchers shot up with the speed of infants wishing to please a new teacher on the first day of term. Others in the ranks behind seemed to have gone to sleep, so Crathorne turned and glowered at them, which seemed to galvanise some into relative wakefulness and gradually more hands went up. Thinking this might not be enough to carry the day one anxious councillor put up both hands in a frantic effort to please but was restrained by his neighbour.

"A-gainst" bellowed Crathorne triumphantly. Six LibDem hands reached for the gargoyles. "Ha ha" chortled Crathorne "I told you so. Sucks to you, ya stupid bitch. Whadda yeh say, eh lads?"

"Arrr, arrr " the dummies muttered in ragged unison, the taste of brown ale already on their lips. Council Chief Executive Colin Shearsmith stood up and started to babble in council-speak. Everything was going according to the five-year plan, apparently. He praised Councillor Crathorne for his honesty, integrity, sound judgement and diligence in serving the people of Durham City. Was it my imagination or was his nose really getting longer and longer? In desperation I looked around for the white rabbit in a black top hat that would complete the pantomime scenario. Beside me the Cobbler could take no more and seemed to explode to his feet like a firework.

"This is just a load of old bullshit" he warned. "Why don't you resign and stop embarrassing the people of Durham, Shearsmith?" For one moment the room was suspended in pin-drop silence, then chaos broke out.

Maurice Crathorne was on his feet shaking his fist at the Cobbler, red-faced with impotent fury. "Eject that person immediately, get him out of here!" the Mayor shrieked at the top of his voice. Pushing their way apologetically through the crowd two elderly gentlemen in red and gold costume hobbled forward on their walking sticks, eager to carry out the Mayor's command. Eventually one of them reached the Cobbler and laid an arthritic hand on his shoulder.

"I, I, I'm v very s sorry, y y y you'll have to g g go" his voice trembled. "The M M Mayor is very upset." The Cobbler looked at this ancient guardian of the Mayor's peace and was about to argue, but in the dimmed lights he noticed a strong resemblance to his great grandfather in the withered face and thought better of it.

Mortally afraid that any loud noises might precipitate a heart attack in this venerable gentleman, he thanked him then turned quietly and left the Council Chamber. Colin Shearsmith appeared visibly relieved at his exit and for the rest of the meeting you could see him casting furtive glances towards the doorway as if afraid that his arch-enemy might return. Unfortunately for the onlookers he did not and the rest of the proceedings passed uneventfully.

The meeting over, we all trooped down the worn stone stairs of the Town Hall, having witnessed Durham democracy in action. The stars were bright and the air fresh. My relief was short-lived, because when I reached the car park somebody has taken a half-brick to the back window of my car and stolen the radio.

Oh joy, Oh rapture.

City Council Elections, May 1st 2003- The Bloodbath

Tony the Cobbler had been threatened that if he stood in the election there would be trouble, and he knew Durham well enough not to ignore threats like that, particularly when they came from the mouth of a uniformed policeman. The only redress he had was to publish photos of Councillors he believed to be corrupt in his window, along with the crimes of which they were guilty. All The Usual Suspects were there, but pride of place was reserved for a photo of John Bowman with his arm around Mildred Brown. Joe Knight, Mick Bennett, Steve Laverick were all left with more time to spend with their families after feeling The Wrath of Cob. The only one to survive the onslaught was the most corrupt of all, foxy Morris Crathorne, scraped through by the skin of his teeth.

The scene at the count was memorable. Time and time again Morris' phone rang "Morris, We've just lost Belmont......Morris, ...we've just lost Gilesgate......Morris......we've just lost Sherburn...." Morris looked deflated at this, the loss of the greatest Labour stronghold, spiritual home of The Usual Suspects. Head in hands, nearby candidates heard him mutter "That bastard Cobbler......" It might be a coincidence that on the following two Saturdays, Northern Echo newspapers disappeared from the paper shops in Sherburn and somehow ended up being burned on a field nearby.

132

Chapter 11
The Standards Board of England

When politicians get themselves into trouble a common way of squirming out of it is to get somebody within the legal profession to have some sort of meeting then write some sort of report saying that they have done nothing wrong. Tony Blair did it with the Hutton Report, but there is a version of this trick that even the humblest Councillor can use. It is called the Standards Board of England.

The Standards Board of England is a new organisation set up by New Labour for the specific purpose of investigating complaints brought by the public against their local councillors. Although its stated intention is that it is meant to be an open and transparent means of investigating complaints about local government malpractice, much of its working practices remain shrouded in mystery, not the least of which is why everybody you speak to on the telephone appears to have a strong Australian accent.

I have allocated a full chapter to the workings of this organisation because it seems to have introduced a new concept to our society, the concept of **inbuilt ineffectiveness;** ineffectiveness that is engineered into the organisation quite deliberately for a specific purpose. Let me explain all about **inbuilt ineffectiveness**. I want you to imagine that you were going to genetically modify a dog so that it looked like a big fierce watchdog, but in reality it was no use whatsoever for that purpose.

The first thing you would have to do would be to get rid of those nasty sharp white things in its mouth because you wouldn't want your watchdog biting anybody. That bark has got to go as well. After all you might frighten some ageing burglar to death and you wouldn't want that, would you? Restricted mobility, a friendly nature that belies its savage appearance and a nice glossy coat would be added advantageous features. There you have it, a watchdog that looks great but in reality is no f*cking use whatsoever. That, ladies and gentlemen, is the Standards Board of England.

What is the Standards Board of England meant to do? The Standards Board is an organisation set and run up by the Office of the Deputy Prime Minister (yes, John Prescott) and meant to be an open and independent way of investigating allegations of corruption among local politicians. In fact it is exactly the opposite, **It is a way of making sure that only the complaints that politicians want to have**

investigated get investigated.

Theoretically speaking a book like this one should not be necessary because if a local politician does something wrong you could make a complaint to the Standards Board and the Board will come and sort it out with their special team of investigators. I have their complaints leaflet in front of me now, entitled "Councillors behaving badly?" with a Blairite-looking young man, arms folded, staring at the slogan at the bottom of the cover that says "Confidence in Local Democracy." Hang on, am I imagining something or are his lips moving? Yes, he's saying something- if you put your ear to the cover you can just hear it. **" Don't bother mate, this is just one big con-trick. You might as well save your time and stamp money"**

Let me read the first paragraph of their glossy little brochure. **"1. What does the Standards Board do? We were set up under the Local Government Act 2000 and are independent of the government."** Hang on, I thought you said it was run by John Prescott's office? - shut up I'm reading! **"We investigate written complaints of misconduct by councillors in local government and other authorities listed in section 7 of this leaflet. Our investigators, known as Ethical Standards Officers (ESOs), have extensive powers, allowing them to investigate matters thoroughly and without bias. There is no charge for our service."** Well it looks as if Prescott has missed out on a canny little money earner here, why doesn't he charge for the service? - That's probably waiting until after they get their Third Term in Office and they privatise it, you know what I mean? PFI, great big offices built by their mates at exorbitant prices, massive salary increases for directors, that sort of thing. Hey look, you can get this booklet in Braille, on tape, in Cantonese and Swahili.....

Right, what's this **inbuilt ineffectiveness** about that you were telling us before? Ok, let me explain. The fact is, you don't want anybody finding out just how corrupt local Labour Councillors are, so you set up this organisation to cover it all up. The first step is that you appoint these guys and call them **Ethical Standards Officers**. There are only a very small number of them, only 39 to cover the whole country in fact, and there are thousands of complaints so the government can justify giving the Standards Board the power to prioritise the complaints they receive. They can decide that a complaint is too trivial to investigate, and does not need to be sent to the overworked Ethical Standards Officers.

They can also decide to send it down any number of treacherous legal dead-ends within the Local Government Act 2000 and they do not need to give a detailed reason for their decision, because there is no appeals process. This is State-of-the Art use of the law to deny justice to the ordinary man or woman in the street, and I have absolutely no doubt that Blair, Straw and all the other devious lawyers within New Labour are very proud of their achievement.

Yes, there is an open and independent system for the investigation of complaints, but I'm sorry mate, your complaint hasn't quite made it that far. It's gone into the bin like most complaints do. What proportion? Well you can never tell because your complaint has not actually gone into the system, it's been weeded out by the pre-complaints procedure so the details don't appear on the website. The Board themselves admit that something like 75% to 90% of all complaints go this way. No appeals process, so just bend over, put your head between your legs and kiss all possibilities of justice goodbye. Of course you can ask for a judicial revue and take it to court, but your case has been weakened by the fact that it has already been investigated by the proper process set up under the Local Government Act 2000 and found to be without merit, therefore it is unlikely that you will get legal aid to help you

If, due to some unforeseen circumstances, your complaint does get as far as the Ethical Standards Officers, (and I have yet to meet anybody who has managed this feat) you will find that the punishment they can dole out to guilty councillors is very limited indeed. Unlike the previous system where, for instance, a district auditor could surcharge a councillor for financial malpractice, **the Standards Board can only suspend councillors from office.** Any financial redress has to be done separately through the aforementioned court of law. Look carefully into the great slavering mouth of our Standards Board watchdog and you will find the complete absence of any sharp tooth-like object. Even the gums are specially softened so it cannot even give corrupt councillors a nasty suck, and that is the way it is meant to be. This is a process with **inbuilt ineffectiveness**, specially set up by politicians to protect other politicians. What use is a complaints process when its decisions depend not upon whether or not a misdemeanour has taken place, but upon who has made the misdemeanour?

So important is this new concept of **inbuilt ineffectiveness** that I suggest we set up a permanent memorial to it within the English language. If we want to deride something as useless, what do we compare it to? A chocolate fireguard or a chocolate teapot. This is totally anachronistic, we are no longer living in the comfortable age of open fires and teapots. I am suggesting a new phrase especially for the New Labour era., and here it is. **"You're about as much use as the Standards Board of England."** Here's one possible example of how it might be used from the terraces of the Stadium of Light in Sunderland during a football match.

"Hey did you see that blatant foul there? The referee must be blind. Referee- are you blind? **You're about as much bloody use as the Standards Board of England**."

A little bit of improvisation is acceptable. For instance "Get off the pitch referee - we might as well have an Ethical Standards Officer out there for all the good you are" is a possibility. Of course once you master the whole concept then you can really go to town. How about something like this for when your team has just been beaten thoroughly and you are really disillusioned. The following might be appropriate:

"That team is about as much use as the Standards Board of England. They are, they're about as much use as a bunch of Australian bloody lawyers, brought over here for no apparent bloody reason by John Prescott - My God, John Prescott, what a tosser, don't we have enough shady lawyers in this country without him bringing more over from Australia?- sitting in their fancy bloody offices, being paid loads of taxpayers' money for trying to pull the f*cking wool over our eyes, trying to con us that there's an independent way of investigating complaints against f*cking councillors when it's just a big f*cking con. Neither use nor f*cking ornament the lot of them"
Get the idea?

Apparently I'm not the only one who is concerned about the ethical standards of our Ethical Standards Officers. Here's an e-mail I got recently from somebody I met in the Cobbler's shop who has also tried to get the Standards Board to investigate a complaint:

"You might want to take a look at the workings of the Standards Board of England which has just been set up to investigate complaints about the behaviour of local councillors. From what I can see it is a way of preventing allegations against politicians being investigated rather than actually investigating them. Allegations go to The Standards Board, which then acts as a sort of black hole. Investigators (for want of a better word) seem to look first and foremost for reasons why they should not investigate the allegations if at all possible.

I have come across a lot of complaints about local politicians in Durham City which are backed by good evidence, and the Standards Board have simply dismissed them on technicalities. I first became suspicious of this organisation when it became obvious that politicians themselves were keen to have allegations against them investigated by The Standards Board (see www.standardsboard.co.uk)

Upon phoning the Standards Board yesterday afternoon, I was rather surprised to find out that everybody there seems to be from Australia. Is there a reason for this? - *the imagination starts to wander while being put on hold. The Standards Board is run by John Prescott. Could this have anything to do with it? You know what he's like. Could they all be his children, the result of passionate nights of shore leave while he was a merchant seaman? Sudden mental picture of John Prescott fornicating with an equally large Australian female who looks not unlike a kangaroo from the rear. Horrible sight- I don't know what the kangaroo sees in him.*

Fortunately I was dragged back to reality at this point by another female voice with a thick Australian accent

"Gerdie, kernie helpya?" the voice on the line enquired. Yes, I replied, I wanted to know why all of the complaints passed to me had been knocked on the head straight away without any proper investigation. "Shural putchya throotatha legal people." *Legal people - does that mean that there are also illegal people there ?- that's it.- illegal immigrants- A PFI sort of thing.*

Hang on, back to reality. I've got the legal department on the line. The answers I received from the legal department member were also in a thick Australian accent, which hampered communication considerably . The fact that I cannot understand English speaking lawyers does not help, of course. The understanding I think I eventually reached was that at least 75% of the complaints received the urgent attention of a Catholic priest, because they ended up in a pigeon-hole labelled *Now Father Eggshun.*

"Who is Father Eggshun, can I talk to him? I asked.

"Now, now Father Eggshun" the voice retorted somewhat sharply.

"So who's Father Eggshun?" I ask again.

The voice at the other end of the telephone is even more strident. "Now sah, ya don't seemta unnastand. Now father eggshun. We do not intend to take any father eggshun with respect to your complaint." At last comprehension dawns. Father Eggshun is actually a gigantic wastepaper basket with an Australian lawyer at the other side of the room, screwing the complaints up into a ball and throwing them into a wastepaper basket. "Now father eggshun..... Now father eggshun..... Now father eggshun..... Hey, look Joe I just gotta tin-outa-tin there!"

The rest of the conversation led me to believe that the remainder of the complaints received some sort of complex re-assignment between four categories, the details of which quickly baffled me (in fact I suspect that was the whole idea) but I brightened up when I heard about the "Audi - pee". Interest wained again when I found out that we were not talking about some sort of incontinent motorcar, the lady was actually referring to the ODP, an abbreviation for the Office of the Deputy Prime Minister.

As I understand it (actually I don't) if the Standards Board cannot find any other way of knocking an allegation on the head they assign it to Category C, which (I think) means Local Adjudication. Unfortunately, (I believe) local adjudication regulations are not yet in place in Durham, possibly due to the (in)activities of Two-Jags at the Audi-pee. This means (I think) that the matter then goes into the "Now Father Eggshun" black hole, but my enlightenment was cut short because the lady at the other end of the line was getting anxious about the time. "Look sah, I'm a lawyer, and it's parst my time ta go howm." Yes, it was 5.33 pm.

"Can I come to your second annual meeting next week?" I ask. "Sure, I'll put ya through. It costs money, mind." I am put on hold for a minute or so, then. "I'm sorry sah, we stopped taking bookings for the conference last week" says another voice from down-under "Gabye." You can almost hear him at the other end of the line saying "Ah well, that's got rid of another winging Pommy b*stard!".

I know a lot of people from Durham who have made complaints to the Standards Board, so why are there no allegations for Durham under the "D" section on the website?

The Standards Board of England needs further investigation"

There you go then. I am not the only person who is complaining about the Standards Board of England. I'm not a lone, isolated paranoid nutter, am I? Am I? Please, somebody talk to me, please......."

Incidentally, if your complaint is not about the elected councillors, but the full-time council employed officers, then you need to be talking to the Local Government Ombudsman. Strangely enough, it is also run by the Office of the Deputy Prime

Minister, John Prescott. Oh no, I just can't take any more………

MP's are above all of this, of course. Their activities are controlled by the Parliamentary Ombudsman. Interestingly, Parliament has the power to sack the Parliamentary Ombudsman if it does not like what the Ombudsman is doing, an enviable situation shared, to my knowledge, by no other workforce. Elizabeth Filkin, the Parliamentary Ombudsman who revealed misdeeds by Keith Vaz and Peter Mandelson and thereby caused their downfall as Ministers was not sacked, but her hours and staff were reduced and her life made so difficult that eventually she resigned. How do you become an MP, anyway? Mail me the application forms straight away.

Update 25th November 2003

The England Rugby Squad come home with the Webb Ellis Trophy. Ah well, that's one up for the whinging Poms, then. I think I'll phone the Standards Board up and say "Fancy a game of rugby, mate?"

Chapter 12
In the Beginning…..

You might be wondering, dear reader, what a chapter entitled "In the Beginning…." is doing at the end of a book. Well, even as the author I am not sure myself. All I do is go down and talk to the man as he hammers away at the shoes and serves his customers, and then go away and try to write down what he says. That in itself is not always easy because as likely as not some good-looking young lady has just come into the shop and fluttered her eyelashes at him and he has just promised to do her shoes straight away. So now he is working away like crazy, talking through a mouthful of nails and banging away at a pair of shoes as I try to communicate with him. The scene is often something like this.

"Listen, all that stuff you brought in yesterday is just mmm…. a load of old BANG BANG BANG BANG BANG not even listening to what I BANG BANG BANG BANG BANG. It was Mildred and BANG BANG BANG BANG BANG with a mmmm…cucumber not a candle BANG BANG BANG BANG BANG round the other end and mmmm…she didn't like it at all, so then BANG BANG BANG BANG BANG…."

"What do you say, I didn't catch that with all the hammering?" I ask.

"I said you're not BANG BANG BANG BANG BANG tell ya at all , are you? Listen, mmm…it was BANG BANG BANG BANG BANG." Suddenly the attractive young lady walks into the shop. His eyes light up. "Hiya, darling, they'll be ready in a minute, just hang on." BANG BANG BANG BANG BANG.

"I'll come back later when you're not quite so busy, Tony"

"Whadaya BANG BANG BANG BANG BANG?"

In despair I leave the Cobbler's shop. I have been in there about five minutes and by now the traffic wardens have almost certainly put another one of their expensive little messages onto my car' which is parked in the loading area about twenty yards down from the shop because there is not one single parking space to be had for miles around. I think that this chapter is meant to be all about how his difficult upbringing in Newcastle was the catalyst that turned him into the person he is now.

As I understand it, Tony was born in October 1963 at Pottery Bank which is in Walker Road, Newcastle. This is the roughest part of a rough area, and in those circumstances you learn how to fight before you learn how to walk, because fighting is a natural part of your life. The fact is that much the same could be said of many of his Labour Party opposition who were veterans of the pits of the Durham coalfield and even fought in the Korean War during their period of National Service. The only thing you can say with any degree of certainty is that when people with this sort of background come into opposition, sparks are going to fly.

It wasn't that Tony had any sort of political axe to grind, and you do not have to know him very long before you realise that he has no interest in politics, he is simply relentless in exposing corruption no matter what political party is involved. Those who go into the shop are unaware of the real toll that this struggle has had on him and his family, because his ever-optimistic manner disguises it. You need to know him really well before he starts talking about his father's nervous breakdown after the police surveillance operation on the shop, and the times of self-doubt when the situation was so overwhelming that the only thing he could do was to drive over to the quiet shores next to Priory Castle, and look out over the sea as he mulled over the events of the day, screaming inside his head. Could he really be right, and everybody else in the world wrong?

The thing that kept him going was the fact that a lot of his predictions about the dire state of the Council's finances would only get worse unless they did something about it came true. During an interview with Mike Parr on Radio Newcastle he predicted that the Gala Theatre could not succeed almost five months before it opened, and Mike Parr shot him down. What the journlist did not know, and the Cobber could not say on air was that he had inside information that alleged the Council had falsified to the Millenium Commission the extent of their matching funds, to the tune of around £2 million. In another prediction on Close Up North he stated that he would bring Durham City Council down, promising to remove Colin Shearsmith from office in disgrace. Both have happened. There are people with Ecomics Degrees who are paid a lot of money and would envy the ability to make predictions of this accuracy.

Having said all of that, the local Labour Party seem to have brought a lot of the trouble on themselves by their own arrogance. President Roosevelt is alleged to have said of one dissenting ex-supporter "Do we want this guy inside the tent pissing out, or outside the tent pissing in?" The fact is that City of Durham Constituency Labour Party pissed off so many of its supporters that there were so many people outside of their tent pissing in that their combined urination, arching in a great steaming yellow-tinged rainbow from the Cobbler's shop across and down the street into the Claypath Labour Club, drowned the Council. I appreciate that this is not a pretty metaphor, but there are so many ex-Labour activists who say that they only got what was coming to them.

Nobody in their right minds creates the sort of chaos they did with their crazy parking restrictions, and then goads the public by voting free parking for the councillors on the same day that they voted to end free disabled parking. Only a party that has lost touch with the electorate completely would do that, thanks to your leaking the facts to the press. Also the disillusionment with the national Labour Party did not help, but the result in Durham City was an exceptionally bad one. So bad that Mick Hills at Labour North announced that they were going to hold a post-mortem about the way that the local party had run the election and invite the Cobbler to contribute his side of the story. Unfortunately, like most Labour promises it did not happen.

In my view, the way the Cobbler finally screwed Durham City Council was by keeping dissent alive. The way the briefcase criminals work is to attempt to isolate any dissenting individual, trying to keep them apart from others with a similar complaint. Eventually, after months and months of delay have stretched into years and years of delay, even the most strident complainant starts to believe that he or she is indeed an isolated, crazy malcontent and stops complaining. Go into the Cobbler's shop with a complaint against the Council and in all probability you will leave with the telephone number of at least one other person with a similar complaint. That person then realises that they are not alone and it gives them heart to keep on fighting.

The Cobbler's best weapon is, of course, his famous shop window. The double yellow lines and traffic lights outside the shop which started the dispute have turned into a blessing in disguise because you can see what happens when cars and buses are stopped by a red light. All eyes turn towards that shop window to see if there has been an update, and a lot of those passengers make a mental note to make the Cobbler's shop window part of their next trip to Durham City so they can read the small print of the incriminating documents in it. Of course a lot of the newspaper clippings in the window are a result of the Cobbler's activities themselves, because his extensive paper database on the wall at the back of the shop includes a lot of journalists just waiting for the next juicy bit of scandal to come their way, courtesy of the Cobbler's mobile phone.

For instance, it seems strange that the Cobbler's revelation that Durham City Councillors had voted themselves free parking at the same time as cancelling disabled parking sparked the front page headline "Hypocrites!" in the Evening Chronicle, but it was never mentioned in the Northern Echo or Durham Advertiser. All I can say is that if you read only the Durham Advertiser and the Evening Chronicle and you think you know what is going on in Durham City, then I suggest you think again. If the things published in the Cobbler's window were untrue then he would have been sued over and over again. John Bowman and Maurice Crathorne have threatened to sue him, but never quite got around to it. I wonder why?

It may or may not be simply a coincidence that the Northern Echo and Durham Advertiser carried such muted coverage of Labour sleaze while reporting on the infamous Claypath land deal to the rear of 18 Claypath. As part of this deal Robert Fulton sold land to the rear of 18 Claypath to the City Council and got land in South Street, Ruth First House (the old Planning Office) and several shops in Claypath from the Council in return. Guess who were Robert Fulton's tenants in 18 Claypath? Well, none other than your friendly local Northern Echo and Durham Advertiser, of course. It gets even better, because guess where the Northern Echo and Durham Advertiser's new offices are? Ruth First House, of course - it's a funny old world at times, isn't it?

And it's getting funnier by the minute. At the centre of the infamous Ransom Strip deal that sparked the whole controversy off was the fact that it seems that this ransom strip was created deliberately. Most people buy land first and then build on it. In this case the council bought most, but not all, of the land, started building on it, then started wringing their hands in pseudo-grief because they were being charged a lot of money for a bit of land they needed, but had inadvertently forgotten to buy. This was the so-called Ransom Strip, and I remember Gerry Steinberg himself defending the massive charge that the Council was being forced to pay on the grounds that the Council themselves were prone to holding others to ransom in a similar way whenever the occasion demanded it

Now remember the incident described earlier in this book when the Cobbler tells us that he was threatened by a police constable in uniform that if he knew what was good for him he would not stand as a candidate in the City Council elections. Knowing as the Cobbler did how the police had hindered the investigation of the anonymous telephone death threats against him, he withheld his nomination until the police had investigated this second threat. The investigation was delayed until after the deadline for nominations to be received. Put yourself in his place and ask

143

yourself whether to continue with his campaign under those circumstances would have been bravery, or would it have crossed over the border into foolhardiness?

Are we living in a democracy or not, Mr Steinberg? If this sort of thing were going on in South Africa you would be the first to condemn it. It is happening in your constituency and it is being covered up. Why?

There were a large number of people in Durham City who were in no doubt whatsoever that the Cobbler was largely instrumental in the downfall of Labour-controlled Durham City Council. On Friday May 2nd, the day after the election when the truth dawned on the electorate of Durham that the party that had ruled Durham City for as long as anybody could remember had been defeated, he could hardly find time to chew a mouthful of nails with people of all political persuasions coming into his shop to congratulate him. All day long there were cars hooting their horns and waves from the occupants and it was days before the clamour subsided.

It is now almost a year since that fateful day and the big question mark that hangs over Durham City Council is "has anything really changed, apart from Labour red turning to LibDem yellow?" Sadly, for many of us the answer is "Apparently not." The LibDems have overturned a long political tradition and their sights are set upon the County Council and Parliamentary seats that are up for re-election in eighteen months' time. If, as I suspect, Durham is a microcosm of the national political situation then the next eighteen months are going to be absolutely critical for the LibDems. They tell us that they are serious about replacing the Tories as the real party of opposition for Labour, but we all know that what they are really after is to form a historic first LibDem national government. The reality of the situation is that they have got to convince the voters that it will be worth their while to put their crosses next to the soaring bird logo. Nothing I have seen so far in Durham would lead me to believe that this is a worthwhile option.

Here then are ten questions for LibDem Leader Sue Pitts, and if she provides me with satisfactory answers I will vote LibDem, otherwise I will join the growing trend and simply stay at home

1) At the very end of the BBC Close Up North Documentary of which Cobbler Tony Martin was the subject, reference was made to new information relating to council purchases of cleaning materials at inflated prices. This has come to be known as the "Ultra Clean Scam" and that two gentlemen by the names of Thomas Purton and Jeff Riddell have been implicated in this apparent fraud. Why, in spite of this very public

exposure, has no attempt been made to investigate this and do you intend that this wholly unsatisfactory state of affairs should continue?

2) Ex-council leader Maurice Crathorne seems to have appointed an extraordinary number of his own relatives to positions of responsibility within the council during his time in office. Since you took over leadership of the Council have you made any attempt to establish whether or not these appointments were made because the recipients deserved them, and that there is no suspicion of nepotism?

3) There is a tremendous amount of unresolved uncertainty about the way that the £1 million contract for the large format film "A Sacred Journey" was awarded to Dr Brendan Quayle. Why was Doctor Quayle given money by the Council before the tendering process, such as it was, began? It seems that without this initial financial help from Durham City Council Dr Quayle would not have been in a position to tender for the film. Furthermore, contrary to statements which were subsequently made by Durham City Council there were other organisations that were able and willing to undertake production of large format or I-max films who were not invited to tender for this film, and this was clearly contrary to the Compulsory Competitive Tendering procedures which were normal practice within the Council at the time. Now that the film has been shown for more than a year it has proved an extremely bad investment for the council taxpayers of Durham City, and it is quite clear that spending £1 million on a venture of this sort was extremely unwise. What steps have you taken to investigate these irregularities, and to make sure that repetitions of this costly error do not take place in the future? CEO Colin Shearsmith must take responsibility for his central role in the decision-making in relation to this debacle. Has he been subjected to any disciplinary procedures, or is it likely that he will receive any retraining in the near future to prevent a reoccurrence of events like this while he remains in post? A great deal of money could have been returned to Durham City Council by activation of claw-back clauses. Why has this not been done? While you were in opposition Ms Lesley Blackie told Grenville Holland in relation to the "Sacred Journey" scandal that "the only way you would get this information is by suing me." Has anything changed since you gained power?

4) The Millennium City development appears to be heading towards the same financial disaster as the Gala Theatre. When is it your intention to

inform the public of the true facts in relation to these developments? Is the public aware that they are unwittingly subsidising the Gala Theatre to the extent of approximately £900,000 per year and that the Millennium City development is still in its infancy yet it is £2 million overspent. Where has all of this money gone?

5) At the last full meeting of Durham City Council before the election in May 2003 a member of the public, who is now a LibDem councillor and senior member of your cabinet, questioned the propriety of the proceedings in that no Treasurer's Report was presented, which under the circumstances was highly unusual. The suspicion remains that a great deal of public assets were sold off in the months leading up to that election. When do you intend to tell the public exactly what was sold off at that time, and where has the money gone?

6) It is clear that there have been many occasions over the past few years, including the time when you yourself were part of the inner cabinet of Durham City Council, when the behaviour of many of your fellow councillors fell below that which the public were entitled to expect. For instance it is known that you are aware of the fact that Councillor John Bowman fraudulently claimed expenses for both City Council meetings and Healthcare Trust meetings, which he could not have attended because they occurred at the same time. You have stated that your reason for not making that information available to the police so that they can decide whether or not to prosecute is that "he only did it four or five times." Other sources lead us to believe that this crime was revealed to a meeting of City of Durham Constituency Labour Party, that the sum in question is at least £7000 and possibly twice that amount, which is much more than could be expected from false claims relating to such a small number of meetings. Furthermore you have information relating to bullying and inappropriate behaviour of City Councillors, including Councillor Bowman, in their capacity of governors of Belmont Comprehensive School under the chairmanship of Councillor Bowman's brother-in-law Councillor Ray Pye. A folder containing documentation has been placed in the hands of a LibDem City and County councillor who is also a governor of Belmont Comprehensive School. Included in this file is evidence that shows that a member of staff, namely Mrs Christine Walker Jones, was incapacitated by an assault by a pupil but was unable to obtain compensation because of the inappropriate conduct of the governing body, and her only redress was to publish the facts of her case in a double-page spread in the Mail on

Sunday. Once again nothing has been done by you to investigate these allegations. Is it your intention that abuses of this sort should continue to go unchecked?

7) Central to cover-ups such as Councillor Bowman's fraud is City Council solicitor Lesley Blackie. I am aware that this lady has refused to provide accounts to the public and police might throw some light upon this matter, even though there is a statutory requirement for her to do so. Further concern is raised by the fact that Ms Blackie has had sight of information relating to suspicious activities of a taxi company involving Councillor Maurice Crathorne's brother-in-law, and no action has been taken in respect of this either. Is it your intention that this unsatisfactory situation should continue now that you have the power to order this lady to provide this information to the public, or do you intend to fulfil your promise made to the public immediately after your election victory and do something about corruption within Durham City Council?

8) Senior Recreation Officer Lynn Danby was allowed to resign after being caught stealing from the Council, in spite of the fact that several council employees including Treasurer Liz Hall witnessed her offence. Her predecessor Keith Walton was also allowed to resign after committing gross misconduct. In view of this, is it not time for the Council to reassess not only the disciplinary procedures but also the selection procedures for this grade of council officer? We are told by several sources that Lynn Danby was allowed to resign rather than being dismissed because she threatened to "open her mouth about everything." What information does this grade of officer have that appears to render them immune to the penalty of instant dismissal which would no doubt be applied to an officer of lower status for similar offences?

9) Information I have received from Durham Land Registry in relation to the sale of 16 Whinney Hill in June 2002 by Durham City Council (Title Number DU253353) is of particular concern to me, even on the basis of the limited amount of information I have at present. It is quite clear that the sale price of £63,000 was well below the market value for a property of this sort. What steps have you taken to ensure that council property is sold in the correct way, and at an appropriate price? How can I, as a member of the public, go about finding out whether this was an isolated incident or one of a series of similar incidents?

10) A great deal of concern is being expressed about the performance of City Council Chief Executive Colin Shearsmith. Even on the basis of the limited information available to me, there appears to be a valid reason to review the criteria for the assessment of this man's performance in this very senior post within the council. His management style has been questioned as "secretive" by a local government ombudsman in recent times, and it would appear that on occasions the reports he presents to the members do not portray the situations he describes with the necessary degree of accuracy. This same criticism has been expressed in relation to his dealings during the "Sacred Journey" contract, when he appears to have acted with an undue amount of autonomy, and to my knowledge you have received information from a former member of the Entertainment Team (Durham) Limited which criticises Mr Shearsmith similarly in respect of other aspects of the Gala Theatre debacle. Is it your intention to review Mr Shearsmith's performance and perhaps assess his need for retraining? Do you intend to monitor his performance more closely in the future? Do you intend to make the voters of Durham aware of the massive financial repercussions that this man's decisions will have for them in the future?

It's up to you now Sue. You were given the mandate by the voters of Durham on 1st May 2003. Show us all, are you the new broom that is going to sweep Durham City Council clean, or are you just the Pitts?

That was the letter that the Cobbler sent to the LibDem leader. Her reply was simple and straightforward. The message was "Sorry, we are looking forward, not back. All is forgiven, no investigations. Yours faithfully, Sue Pitts. "

There were all sorts of ramifications associated with the publication of these questions which Ms Pitts refused to answer. Further information has become available relating to the question concerning Lynn Danby and her resignation from her Senior Recreation Officer's post. It has been alleged that staff from the City's Recreation Facilities have been called into the offices at the old Tourist Information Centre and briefed by a LibDem councillor on how to evade questions about the events leading up to Lynn Danby's resignation. Why is an elected councillor, who should not have anything to do with staffing matters, doing this? More corroborative evidence has been passed to the Cobbler concerning Thomas Punton and Jeff Riddell, implicated in the Ultraclean scam, and a report from the Director of Corporate Finance who seem to have compiled a false report concerning these allegations.

Work was carried out at a property belonging to Mr Thubron at Kelloe, who was related to Mr Punton. The Council charged him £3,078 inc vat on April 21st 2000, and the Council state that they made a small profit from it, which was returned to the Highways accounts. Lies!.......Closer investigation of the bill shows that two labourers and brickies were employed for thirteen days, which itself amounted to £3,000. As well as that £1,000 was paid for a JCB, £1,600 for the tarmac, £400 for dolomite, £1,350 to lay the kerbstones, £800 to hire a wagon.........the list goes on and on. These prices are exclusive of VAT! The true cost was well over £10,000, and there are witnesses to all of this. This evidence has been handed over to Sue Pitts. Will she do anything? Only time will tell.

This story only really got interesting in the last few months of writing it, and rather than doing an extensive re-write every time something new came in, eventually I was reduced to sticking it in here as an update. Enjoy. Remember that this is just the tip of the iceberg.

Update 23rd October 2003

I am intrigued by a national news item about suspicions that two out of the three billion dollars allocated by coalition countries to rebuild the war devastation in Iraq has somehow disappeared down a financial black hole somewhere. A standard issue USA spokesperson denies all of this of course, saying (as they do) that everything is OK because the entire process is entirely transparent, so what are you complaining about? We are complaining about the fact that financial black holes are certainly transparent but they are also so deep that you can never see right down to the bottom of them. Hey, Mr or Mrs American Spokesperson, you didn't happen to see three old guys with Geordie accents busy stuffing their pockets with used five and ten dollar bills while you were looking down that black hole, did you? We haven't seen Shearsmith, Bowman & Crathorne around Durham for a while.

Update - November 3rd 2003

You never have an egg when you really need one, do you? That's what I thought to myself as I left the Cobbler's shop this morning. There, standing just outside the Gala Theatre was John Prescott! Overjoyed by this happy conjunction of my two favourite things, I reached down into my carrier bag but to my intense disappointment eggs must not have been on the shopping list my wife had given me. What's John doing here? Of course, that's it - Labour's solution to the Gala Theatre problem. Put Prescott in charge, wait a while, clear away the debris and sell the land as sites for executive houses. You might not like these Labour people but they are clever!

Evening news proves me wrong again. Big John is here to persuade us that a North East Regional Assembly to be built at Aykley Heads in Durham is A Good Thing. Apparently John wants us to vote yes in the referendum next autumn. No, not the referendum on the European Constitution, we're not having one about that, because that is much too important to allow ordinary people to be part of the decision making process. This is a referendum to ask the people of the northeast whether or not they want another vastly expensive building, another layer of local government, more politicians and a regional assembly whose decisions can be overruled by Westminster.

Well John, you certainly seem to have persuaded those two sixteen year old girls you appeared with on Look North tonight but the rest of us remain unconvinced, especially when you read about the spiralling cost of the Scottish Regional Assembly building that started off with an estimated cost of £40 million and has already cost £400 million. You must know something the rest of us do not however, because they are already levelling the site and laying what seem to be foundations up at Aykley Heads. You haven't been consulting Cherie's fortune teller, have you?

Update 30th January 2004

The question put to Sue Pitts about Crathorne's notorious practice of appointing relatives to City Council jobs suddenly resurfaced as Carol Harris, Crathorne's daughter, was mysteriously appointed as Senior Housing Officer in preference to highly qualified candidates such as a gentleman named Tom Graham. Allegedly Mrs Harris was the least well qualified for the job, but it is not what you know, but who you know in Durham City. This is not the first of this lady's fortuitous promotions, because four years ago when she was appointed as Housing Officer there was a great deal of controversy and a letter, compiled by a member of Durham City Council who had applied and been rejected for this position ended up in the Cobbler's window. Crathorne instituted a witch hunt to find the whistleblower, but without success.

Contrary to their leaflets about openness and transparency, nothing has changed under the LibDems. Cabinet Member Dennis Southwell, a regular visitor to the

150

Cobbler's shop for many years, resigned from the Labour Party in disgust over a point of principle. Tony the Cobbler respected this man whom he had always trusted and believed to be a man of honesty and integrity, even to the point of supporting his election campaign, but unfortunately it would seem that Dennis' moral stance has weakened since his appointment to the Cabinet. When questioned about this dubious appointment he implied that the decision had been made before the LibDems came to power, but since the appointment only happened just before Christmas 2003 and the Libdems came to power in May 2003, there was a discrepancy.

9.30 Friday morning, the Cobbler was serving a customer when he noticed a man and a woman photographing his window. There was nothing unusual in this and the Cobbler went out to greet them. In his hand was an important piece of news that he had not had time to put into the window the night before.

"Take a photo of this, it's going up later today and it's a belter" the Cobbler said as he held the paper up against the window.

"I don't like fiction" the man snarled angrily. Suddenly the Cobbler realised that this guy was larger than he first thought, and clearly was not one of his fan club. The man lunged over and grabbed the poster from the Cobbler's hand. His face contorted as he screwed it up into a ball, and the Cobbler began to wonder just where this guy intended to stick this screwed up ball of paper, because he did not give the impression of being altogether a happy man. However the Cobbler was having none of it and attempted to grab the poster back, and a tug-of-war developed with the woman screaming encouragement while the man jabbed a jagged edge of the camera into the Cobbler's hand.

Eventually the man decided the camera was worth more than the paper and let go. Two batteries dropped out of the camera and the man began fumbling around on the floor for them He retrieved them and as they hurried off the Cobbler bellowed "Do you realise just how much trouble you're in now?"

"You're the one in trouble" the man replied **"Morris is going to sort you out, you're going to get hurt!"**

As the pair scuttled past The Jug, the Cobbler's customer emerged from the shop, obviously shocked. "Are you alright?" she asked.

"Sure" the Cobbler reassured her "That was just a mild attack. Nothing out of the ordinary."

"That was disgraceful. Please take my name and address, and if you need a witness, I will do it." the lady said. The Cobbler took the details, thanked her and returned to his cobbling. The next few days were uneventful, until a phone call from a council whistleblower brought an astounding piece of information.

"Do you know who those two people who caused that fuss outside of the shop - the guy has been bragging about how he sorted you out - **it was Carol Harris, Morris Crathorne's daughter, and her husband."**

It was not long before he was hammering on the door of the newly appointed Chief Exec of Durham City Council Brian Spears, whose chair must still have been warm from the rapid departure of Shearsmith's ample buttocks. The smell of corruption still lingered in Shearsmith's office, as the Cobbler remembers (Are you sure it wasn't just bullshit, Tony?)

"Why has Carol Harris been appointed?" enquired the Cobbler after brief introductions. "Why have you put Morris Crathorne's daughter as Senior Housing Officer?"

Spears' eyes took on the same expression that the Cobbler remembered when Shearsmith was cornered. "Er, um.....It wasn't me" Spears faltered " It was Konochewsky who put her into that position." The smell of bullshit grew stronger and the Cobbler's nose began to twitch. Conveniently the doors were open and there were witnesses.

"Are you still knocking off **** *******?" the Cobbler enquired loudly, noticing that his secretary was hovering behind the door. "The first thing you did was to promote her and move Carol Harris up into her position." Spears squirmed in his chair, Shearsmith-like.

"I do not know what you are talking about, Mr Martin" Spears flustered.

"Do you know that Carol Harris and her husband caused a scene outside of my shop in Council time last Friday? Did you send them up to do it?"

"No" replied Spears, looking remarkably unfazed by the revelation of an assault on a member of the public by a senior Council officer "I'll look into it." He scribbled the allegation onto the end of the long list he already had.

"Why don't you introduce the claw-back clause on Brendan Quayle's film - look at the amount of money it is losing" the Cobbler continued "You could at least get back some of the taxpayers' money. That film is pathetic, have you seen it? You are getting an average of only two people every time it is shown, and Quayle is getting twelve and a quarter percent of that as well as his million pounds payment. If it hadn't been Quayle, would you have invoked the claw-back?"

"I'll look into that, and see if it's still an option" The CEO mumbled as he scribbled furiously.

"Well, you may as well look at the sale of Sherburn depot, as it hasn't been put out to tender" the Cobbler replied.

"The Valuation Office said we could do it" Spears muttered as yet another allegation was added to his growing list.

Whether or not anything will happen to this list, or was he just playing noughts and crosses? Only time will tell but the Cobbler left Spears' office with a sinking feeling that although the name on the office door had changed, nothing else had.

Update 9th February 2004 - The Documentary

Despite the hammering they are taking over the Hutton Report, the BBC screen Rule & Powers allegations against Durham City Council in their "Inside Out" series, and the lengths the producer had to go to were remarkable. The programme had been trailed the week before after a documentary about the visit to Tyneside of Mohammed Ali, but right up until the moment it was broadcast it had to be kept secret and local newspapers stated that the BBC were reluctant to confirm that it was going ahead. Only a small fraction of the footage shot by them was eventually broadcast.

The real meat of the programme was a reconstruction of the infamous " you will not survive" meeting between Shearsmith, Rule & Liz Hall. You can see just how fearful the BBC were by the way they hired somebody to play the part of Shearsmith who was considerably better looking than the real thing. The Durham Advertiser that came out the following Thursday with the headline "Stage Set for Gala New Era" did not even mention the fact that a documentary had been broadcast, but did mention that Joe Anderson, the gritty ex-mayor of Durham demanded a public enquiry.

What the documentary did prove was just how deep the Council cover-up had been. They proved without a doubt that the Council was fully aware of the financial problems that had dogged the theatre from the very start. The saddest part was LibDem City Council Leader Sue Pitts' attempted justification of the massive fraud committed by her Labour predecessors, making no reference to the fact that she was part of the Labour dominated cabinet that had sanctioned it. News was leaking out of a bust-up between senior LibDem Councillors over the cover up, and their leader's lack of openness to her own party about the cover-up.

Meanwhile it was becoming apparent that the size of Shearsmith's golden handshake was becoming an embarrassment. A Councillor whistleblower alleges that the total cost to the taxpayer of getting rid of Shearsmith was a massive £278,000, not counting his £1,000 per week pension. To avoid bankrupting the wages fund the Council has asked for permission from John Prescott's office to capitalise the payment - in other words to call it a one-off expense that can be written off over a number of years. It's all right for some, isn't it? Just before he left Shearsmith sent a memo to all of the staff saying that he had left the Council in a strong financial position and self-praised his own contribution to Durham. In reality, the Council Tax increase, which should have been capped at 6%, is now round about 9% which means that about 3% of your Council tax is doing nothing other than funding his incompetent management of the start-up of the Gala Theatre.

Colin Shearsmith rides off into the sunset, leaving a trail of debt, corruption and bullshit behind him, with his saddlebags crammed full of taxpayers' money. Still hot on his heels is his archenemy The Durham Cobbler. Who was it that said "Crime does not pay?" What a load of cobblers!

The End

....or is it? There are masses of information that we have had to leave out for legal reasons, and more is coming in every day. What can we do with it? The police won't investigate it, the MP won't investigate it, and the LibDems won't investigate it. What we need is a public inquiry of the sort Joe Anderson, ex-mayor and Labour Councillor for thirty years demanded on the front page of last week's Durham Advertiser. Will we get it? Don't hold your breath. The fact is that the only solution is to remove the LibDems and the corrupt Labour-controlled County Council and form our own independent party with no political affiliations, which will act only for the good of the people of Durham. Watch this space, or better still the Cobbler's Window of Truth.

Update 7th March 2004

The authorities seem to be going into panic overdrive about the publication of this book. The Cobbler has just been served a seven day notice to quit. Not much notice after hundreds of years on the site, is it? It sounds a bit suspicious in that the Diocesan refuse to tell Tony exactly how much he owes them and told them that he could pay them with profits from the book, but it was clear from the attitude of the people serving the notice that money was not the real issue here. "We are selling the block and we want to sell it as vacant possession, so we need you out in a week, thank you very much and goodbye."

As you can imaging this was such a shock to Tony that it was several days before he was capable of piecing together the truth. A well known local property developer, allegedly one of The Usual Suspects, has put a bid in to buy the block and turn it into student accommodation and had been enquiring about the block for the last three years. Tony refused to leave on Friday 5th, when the notice was due and was prepared to barricade himself in the shop. In the face of this the Diocesin backed down and agreed to allow him to stay until the end of March. However this does look like the end of the Cobbler's Shop in Claypath. It's only in the movies where the plucky little guy always beats the big guy. Real life is very different, unfortunately.

Chapter 12B
Anatomy of a Stitch-up

"There is no defence against an evil which only the victims and the perpetrators know exists."

Steven Knight - The Brotherhood.

Time after time people have come into the Cobbler's shop describing the injustice they have received at the hands of corrupt organisations of one sort of another, and if you look at them in any detail at all you will see that certain similarities and patterns of behaviour exist in the way that organisations conspire to deny these people justice. In this chapter I have made some sort of attempt to classify these methods so that people can perhaps come to realise that they are being stitched up. Strange as it may seem it is not always as easy to recognise that you are being conspired against as you might imagine. The people who perpetrate this sort of act are very adept at disguising it, possibly because they do it for a living and have been doing so for years.

Before publication this manuscript was read by a man whom I believe to be an honest solicitor, and who was obviously hurt by my frequent references to those within his profession who are somewhat less scrupulous than he is. The manuscript came back covered in warnings and suggestions for improvement, most of which I have adopted, and I thank him once again for his help. However, he took one look at the last two sections of this book and made no other comment apart from something like "The wholesale condemnation of entire professions, although undoubtedly entertaining, detracts from the main theme of the book which is about how power is used to maintain the status quo." Sorry, I have to disagree with you there.

The way that organisations conspire together to deny ordinary people justice, as outlined in these last two chapters, is the mechanism used by unscrupulous people to maintain the power they have, even when they are in the wrong. It seems that it has always been like this and it always will be as long as these injustices are kept secret. That is what a stitch-up is all about. Sadly the honest lawyers are saddled with high-profile members of their profession, such as the Blairs, who have shown an absolute contempt for the concept of truth and until somebody within their profession is prepared to stand up and condemn them for it there is a problem.

What is a stitch-up?

A stitch-up is a situation where a person (or persons) is denied justice by a series of unethical (and frequently illegal) acts. The perpetrator of the stitch-up can call upon a wide variety of influential friends to prevent the victim taking effective action. I like to call this group "The Teflon People" because no matter what you throw at them, nothing sticks. There seems to be an increasing number of Teflon People about unfortunately.

Occasionally there are massive stitch-ups that take place in the full glare of international publicity with thousands of victims. In spite of this the victims can do nothing because the perpetrators are overwhelmingly powerful. The Enron scandal is one such example, and history will probably show that Teflon Tony's Second Gulf War scam was another.

Much more common are individual stitch-ups, where a single person is victimised by one or more large organisations. The victim ends up being branded as isolated and paranoid, a chronic moaner. The situation can go on for years, poisoning every aspect of the victim's life if he chooses to continue fighting. I have discovered about ten within a three-mile radius of Durham City Town Hall. This means that either Durham City is exceptionally corrupt or there are tens of thousands of similar situations in Britain. I am prepared to except either explanation.

How do you know you have been stitched up?

Each stitch-up is different, but if you examine a number of them, then certain patterns emerge.

Look for the progression:

> You are in a situation where an injustice has been done to you.
> You have masses of evidence, but nobody seems to want to see it.
> Nobody appears to believe you.
> You are passed from one person to another (the Pass-The-Parcel game)
> Nobody will investigate your claims
> You write hundreds of letters, without result.
> Your house fills up with folders full of documents.

You are branded as paranoid, isolated, crazy, a chronic moaner.

You lose faith in the people around you.

You write to Tony Blair - he ignores you.

People around you lose faith in you, tired of your obsession with the dispute.

You become paranoid, isolated, crazy, and a chronic moaner.

You write to the Queen - she ignores you.

You give up, or get divorced.

You write a book about it. Nobody wants to publish it.

How far down the list are you?

What are the symptoms of a stitch-up?

Look for the six "D's"

Destroy
Delay
Damage
Deny
Disown
Detach

These are almost always used in combinations. Frequently all are used.

Destroy

The most common variation of this is the Disappearing Document trick. Almost every office has a paper shredder, and it is worth its weight in gold in a stitch-up. Important evidence goes missing with an alarming regularity. In one case that has come to my attention the victim was prevented from making an appeal against a court decision because the court had "inadvertently" destroyed its own records, so beware.

Never give any document to anybody else without photocopying it first. I cannot stress this too strongly. It is surprising just how frequently someone you trust turns out to be working against you, and it is better to be safe than sorry in this world.

The second commonest variation of this is to destroy the victim's credibility. Have they complained of depression or used antidepressant medication in the past? That is clear evidence that they are mentally unstable. Nobody else has complained (so you are told) so you are branded as paranoid, an isolated troublemaker. The world is full of people that no matter how much you do for them, they will never be satisfied. He/she is wasting the time that could be used to help others who are more needy, etc.

Damage

If you cannot destroy it then damage it. Subtly different from destruction, damaging is a slow insidious phase. Action is taken which will damage your reputation, for instance. Until recently people were often "fitted up" as drug users or dealers, but now that drug use is more openly tolerated this no longer has the social sting it used to have. The favourite now appears to be involvement with child pornography. Possession of firearms, an old favourite, remains popular with the police force.

Action may be taken to damage your finances or business. New parking restrictions damage your trade. Council workmen inspect your drains, and find expensive damage, whereas in reality they have created this damage. Solicitors advise you to take action that eventually damages your legal case. The list is endless.

Delay

Possibly the all-time favourite. Everything has a deadline attached to it, even if that deadline is death. Legal claims always have a deadline so look for attempts to push you past it. Look for the symptoms of being passed from one person to another in the hope that eventually you will give up. The overall aim is to put the situation so far in the past that they can say that it happened so long ago they cannot investigate it.

The commonest version of the delay game is played like Pass-The-Parcel, except that on each pass a layer of paper is put on instead of taken off. The person is shunted from one person to another, each denying that it is their responsibility to deal with the matter and referring the complainant to past documentation, which grows and grows as does the lawyer's fees if they are involved, which they probably are. The overall aim is to increase the bill until the complainant dies, buckles under the financial pressure or their sense of grievance diminishes with time and they give up. Pass-The-Parcel is the oldest stitch-up trick in the book but still the best and most effective, because the victim is eventually smothered in a giant snowball of paperwork.

Deny

This is a remarkably effective tool in the face of evidence that they cannot destroy. Find some way of denying that they have seen it. Deny it is valid evidence. Deny that it is their responsibility to look at it and then pass it on to somebody else, thus creating delay. Just deny anything and everything.

Disown

So you think you are a member of that trade union, do you? Are you sure? Do you have receipts for your subscriptions? Are you sure you have not resigned, because they have documents on headed notepaper to say you have.

Have you complained that your solicitor is not doing his job quite as you would like? Be careful, because this could be seen as you lacking confidence in your solicitor's ability. This is a good excuse for the solicitor asking you to take your case elsewhere, often just before an important deadline is due. This means that he cannot be blamed for causing you to fail to meet that deadline.

Detach

This is actually the final stage of the process that starts with branding the person as paranoid, and then going on to detach them from an organisation, or their friends or family. I would have liked to use the word "isolate" here but it does not start with a letter D. The whole idea is to persuade the rest of the world (and ultimately you yourself) that you are the only person who is complaining about this sort of thing, you are a paranoid isolated loner, a chronic moaner etc. That is almost certainly not the case, you are the victim of a crime and you must keep on telling yourself that at all costs. Above all you must avoid allowing the dispute to dominate your life. It can take over your every waking moment and then your personal relationships suffer. If you are not careful you become the isolated paranoid loner that The Teflon People are trying to portray, and that is the first step towards separation, divorce and suicide. If you are in a stitch-up you really do need support around you.

The internet has done a lot to connect people together, and there are newsgroups about a lot of things including injustice and workplace bullying. The problem is that censorship of the internet is remarkably easy, and anything with any real meat about it (such as which High Court judges are associated with the Teflon People, for instance) soon disappears into the "File not found" limbo reserved for uncomfortable cyber-truths. Now you know why Margaret Thatcher did not want any trade union left-wingers at GCHQ, which is now mainly, concerned with monitoring political dissidents inside Britain rather than Britain's external opposition.

Who might stitch you up?

Basically, any big organisation that has access to the Old Boys network, which means most of them. Remember that it is not unusual for someone to be victimised by several organisations at the same time, all pointing out to that person that they are complaining about so many different people at once they must be crazy. They are not crazy, in fact emphasising the number of people that the victim is complaining about is *the* classic stitch-up technique.

Here are some of the most frequent. In no particular order we have:

Solicitors, Barristers & the Law

Everybody jokes about how corrupt lawyers are, but very few realise the size of the problem. The Which? Report on solicitors tells us that **one person in six who goes to a solicitor is so dissatisfied with the service they receive that they eventually complain to the Office of Supervision of Solicitors.** That is a stunning failure rate, twenty times higher than that for comparable professionals such as GP's. Imagine this sort of failure rate transferred to other situations. One loaf in six sold at a baker's shop is inedible and causes food poisoning. One out of every six patients who enters a doctor's surgery dies. One out of every six cars sold refuses to start and has to be returned.

Why is this allowed to go on? Simple - it is all down to self-regulation in the legal profession. Keeping the staffing levels at the Office of Supervision of Solicitors low helps, because that means that a big backlog of complaints develops. Approximately four out of every five solicitors who receive a letter from the OSS simply do not answer it, and they usually get away with it

How does society treat this failure rate? Do we have politicians on TV every day talking about inadequate lawyers in the same way they talk about inadequate teachers, doctors and policemen? No. Of the tens of thousands of complaints received by the Office of Supervision of Solicitors every year, only a handful are ever upheld. For the rest they go on charging the public an average of £120 per hour of a solicitor's time, and perhaps twice that for a barrister's time.

One of the commonest complaints against solicitors is that important documents have got lost. For a profession that relies so heavily upon bits of paper this is totally unacceptable. Keeping pieces of paper safe is simple, you start by buying a filing cabinet and some cardboard folders. You take the client's documents, put them in the folders, write the client's name on the front of the folder and put the folder in the filing cabinet. If the document falls out accidentally, put it back again. Come on you people, this is not rocket science we are talking about.

The problem of corrupt solicitors is nothing new. Stephen Knight in his book "The Brotherhood" (Harper Collins 1983) says "Solicitors are very good at it.......Get your man involved in something legal - it need not be serious - and you have him.' Solicitors...... are 'past masters' at causing endless delays, generating useless paperwork, ignoring instructions, running up immense bills, misleading clients into taking decisions damaging to themselves."

This is a very serious situation. It has always been known that thorough knowledge of the law does not mean that a person is any more likely to obey it, and that morality and legality are two different ballgames. In 2003 it would seem that they are not even in the same ballpark. The Office of Supervision of Solicitors is just as bad as the solicitors themselves, according to a series of "Which" reports. Of course it is, it is run by solicitors! Check out the reports of the incompetence of the OSS at www.unjustis.org.uk.

In early 2004 there was a landmark Appeal Court judgement that says that a judge is still doing his job properly even if he is asleep in court. Bearing in mind that judges have previously dismissed the idea of having even a light-touch appraisal system because it might "lower their esteem in the eyes of the public" and no judge has ever been sacked for incompetence, you have some idea of the problem with our judiciary. Blair wants our legal system to be more like the USA, so how about electing judges here as well?

The Police

Because of the immense amount of power wielded by the police, an honest person being victimised by a corrupt policeman is the nightmare scenario for most people. The immediate consequences are likely to be loss of reputation and even liberty.

Steven Knight says "Police can harass, arrest on false charges, and plant evidence. A businessman in a small community or person in public office arrested for dealing in child pornography, for indecent exposure, or for trafficking in drugs is at the end of the line......He will never work again. Some people have committed suicide after experiences of that kind."

Fortunately for society almost all policeman are honest and hard working, but it does seem that the further up the chain of responsibility you go. the less likely it is you will meet an honest man. At the very highest level, where the police force and the security services interface, then beyond a shadow of a doubt people do die. Even more worrying is the fact that if they chose to do so police authorities can render themselves virtually unaccountable.

The increasing number of deaths in police custody can only be described as a worrying trend.

Politicians

These are the only ones who come anywhere close to rivalling lawyers in the public's perceptions of dishonesty. The problem with being victimised by a corrupt politician is that they have rendered themselves virtually non-accountable. Members of Parliament are accountable to their constituency committees, but the worst that they can do is to deselect them so that they cannot stand at the next election. In parliament they are accountable to the Party's Chief Whip. In the case of a Labour politician, this is a formidable lady called Hilary Armstrong.

I met Ms Armstrong on the eve of the last General Election while she was campaigning in her constituency at Consett. She has the air of a very old-fashioned headmistress with a face, as a Yorkshire friend of mine once said "that you could use to chop firewood." Personally I would not like to get on the wrong side of her, but the only offence she regards as serious enough to warrant investigation is that of voting against a Labour government. An MP cannot be sacked, the worst that can happen is that they are suspended from the House of Commons on full pay for three weeks. In practice MP's are only accountable to the press. This seems to be a common trick associated with New Labour. Set up an organisation to do something in a blaze of publicity, with a website and a lot of glossy brochures all over the place. Tell everybody what it is intended to do, but use legal jargon to disguise the fact that in practice it will do exactly the opposite. The infamous Freedom of Information Act was a good example.

When it was included in the 1997 Labour Election Manifesto, everybody thought it would give us a USA-style Freedom of Information Act, which would force the government to reveal sensitive and embarrassing information about itself. In practice when the UK version, (watered down by Jack Straw and neutered by David Blunkett) comes into effect in 2005 it will make information about the public more readily available to the government, but information about the government will become harder for the public to get at.

Not what the activists were led to believe before the election, Tony!

Incidentally, it is rumoured that the long delay in the implementation of this flagship piece of legislation, first given to David Clark along with the Cabinet post of Chancellor of the Duchy of Lancaster within twenty-four hours of the New Labour victory in 1997, has had to be delayed so long because civil servants are having to sift through mega tonnes of New Labour paperwork, shredding anything they might not want revealing. As above, so below!

The changes in the legal aid system that led to the No-Win-No-Fee ambulance chase we have now, and the changes in the Employment Tribunal Regulations are both examples of the way New Labour has used the law as a means of denying justice to ordinary people rather than delivering it.

No-Win-No-Fee sounds like a good way of reducing the legal aid budget but in practice it is simply a way of preventing awkward cases getting to court. Because of the escalation in lawyers' fees the costs of taking a case to court are astronomical, and law firms usually demand an up-front "insurance" payment. There are only a limited number of insurance companies, and you could well end up seeking insurance from the same people who are insuring the people you are trying to sue. Guess what happens?

People's dissatisfaction with their working conditions, such as stress and bullying managers, means that every year about one job in 250 ends up in an Employment Tribunal, which were originally set up to replace expensive legal action in employment matters. When the numbers started to spiral out of control measures were taken to limit the number of cases. People were only allowed to go to an Employment Tribunal if they had exhausted the internal Grievance Procedure system first.

The catch is that many companies insert a clause in their Grievance Procedures, which means they are an alternative to legal action rather than simply a first step. In other words if you go to Grievance you cannot go to Employment Tribunal about the same matter later. This means they are forced to accept the judgement of the company's internal grievance arrangements, which almost invariably find that the aggrieved employee has no case to answer. If they disagree with this they are then forced to go straight to an expensive legal case funded out of their own pocket.

The law is being used to stitch up ordinary working people, giving them no other option than to enter a legal minefield where money equals power. What most ordinary people fail to realise is that, unlike the USA, most civil cases in the UK are heard by a judge alone. Experience shows that judges are much less likely to find in favour of "the little man" and when they do so the amount of the award is invariably much smaller than that awarded by juries in the USA for equivalent judgements. It goes without saying that one judge is much easier to nobble than twelve jury-people, providing you have the right contacts.

Trade Unions

Trade union hypocrisy has reached an all-time high. Unison and GMB have had scandals where their own officials have harassed their own staff and got away with it, the true scale of ballot-rigging for general secretary elections is coming to light and Britain's biggest teaching union is spending hundreds of thousands of pounds of its members' money to cover up the true scale of the incompetence and corruption among its full-time staff.

In my experience trades unions are one of the most common sources of stitch-ups, but they are very good at hiding the fact. A good trade union rep is worth his weight in gold to you, but a bad one is worth twice that much to your employer, who is much more likely to be able to afford it. The value of a union rests very strongly upon your union rep because what you see is quite often what you get. Remember that trade unions and the Labour Party have always been and will always be part of the same organisation. This presents a tremendous dilemma, especially for public sector unions when Labour is in power, and so much depends upon the people at the top.

One of the most successful pieces of New Labour spin (in my humble opinion) is that somehow New Labour has distanced itself from the trade union movement. In fact nothing could be further from the truth. Under New Labour the trade union movement has become the most effective tool for controlling the workforce any government has ever had. So much of New Labour thinking is based upon Margaret Thatcher's notion that "You do not need tanks and guns to control people. All you need to do is convince them that resistance is futile and they will be compliant."

New Labour has treated the bosses of the large trade unions as part of their new elite, and in return the union bosses keep their membership docile by telling them that industrial action is useless. The membership even contributes money from union funds to New Labour at the same time that New Labour is openly scornful of the trade union movement.

At the grass-roots level this shows itself plainly if you go to any of the internet newsgroups relating to workplace bullying. A common theme is that it is virtually impossible to get the full-time staff of certain unions to take action against employers, even when it is quite plain that they should be doing so. The National Union of Teachers and Unison are frequently mentioned in this respect. Tim Field, who runs the biggest workplace bullying website at www.bullyonline.org <http://www.bullyonline.org> has come out and said this publicly, and is being sued for it by the NUT.

If you read the chapter of this book entitled "A Black Cloud Looms" you will read that the Durham City Unison rep was reluctant to take action relating to Abadun McWilliams allegations of racial abuse by Mildred Brown, the Deputy Leader of Durham City Council because "it will spoil my relationship with the Council." This remarkable attitude is something that you find all of the time, and it is destroying workers' confidence in the trade union movement far more than all of Thatcher's anti-trade union legislation

Union reps are often the worst sorts of false friend and you only realise it when it is far too late. **As with solicitors, never give evidence to a union rep without making a copy of it first.**

Employers

This really follows on from the bit about unions. The top priority of human resources managers is to keep the company going, not to keep you happy. If you do not believe that you are likely to be in for a rude awakening. Fortunately most people realise that and do not trust them.

This is by no means an exclusive list. Just about any organisation can stitch you up if it wants to. The important thing is to recognise what is going on, and act as early as possible.

I've been stitched up - what can I do about it?

The aim of the stitch-up is to isolate you and keep you in a state of disinformation. Mushroom Management - keep them in the dark and feed them bull manure - is the order of the day. It is very tempting to resign from, say, a trade union that is not delivering the goods for you. Don't do that, because that is what they want. The impact of your resignation upon an organisation that has tens of thousands of members is absolutely negligible. Much better to remain inside and make others aware of what is going on. It is very, very difficult to change an organisation from the outside.

It is hard to generalise, because stitch-ups are so diverse in their nature. It is important to recognise the symptoms of a stitch-up at the earliest possible stage, and nip it in the bud before it takes hold if you can. Overall I believe it is your duty to keep on fighting, if not for yourself then for the sake of the next person to go down that path. The aim of a stitch-up is to surround you in an impenetrable barrier of corruption and paperwork in the hope that you will become demoralised and give up. Please do not do that because many of us believe that it is a duty to fight corruption has been placed upon our shoulders because we are strong enough to bear it, and there is strength in numbers

Awareness of stitch-ups is important, because this insidious practice is poisoning the lives of thousands of people in the UK. Working with Tony Martin and people like him has proved to me that one man who has sufficient courage can make a significant difference to the world. He has been an inspiration to me, and that is why I wrote this book. I hope that at least a small amount of that inspiration has been passed on to you, the reader. If it has not then that is my fault as a writer, not the fault of Tony Martin the Cobbler.